C000176842

THE
UNVEILING

What the Book of Revelation Says About our World Today

DAVID FELLINGHAM

malcolm down
PUBLISHING

First published 2020 by Malcolm Down Publishing Ltd
www.malcolmdown.co.uk

24 23 22 21 20   7 6 5 4 3 2 1

British Library Cataloguing in Publication Data
A catalogue record for this book is available from the British Library.

ISBN 978-1-912863-69-3

Cover design by
Art direction by Sarah Grace

Printed in the UK

ENDORSEMENTS

With nearly fifty years of ministry behind him, David Fellingham is well known as a Bible teacher, conference speaker, worship leader, songwriter and author. He has a passion for revival, and for churches to be alive in both Word and Spirit. His latest book, *The Unveiling*, shows how Revelation is relevant to our contemporary world, the church and our personal lives, as it explores such themes as worship, spiritual warfare, and our eternal destiny.

R.T. Kendall
Pastor Westminster Chapel 1977–2002

As soon as I read the manuscript for *The Unveiling*, I knew it would fulfil a unique role in studies on Revelation. Dave provides a clear and concise survey of the main themes of the book, but what really powers it is the combination of stories from a lifetime of ministry illustrating themes in the book, along with a perspective on worship, an important theme in Revelation, drawn from Dave's own experience as a songwriter and internationally respected worship leader. Thoroughly worth reading!

David Campbell, co-author (with G.K. Beale) of *Revelation: A Shorter Commentary* and author of *Mystery Explained: A Simple Guide to Revelation*

The Unveiling is such a timely gift to the church – a thoroughly biblical, yet incredibly accessible, glimpse into one the most misunderstood books. Dave skilfully roots his teaching into the original historical context – as well as allowing the text to come alive for today's turbulent times. This book is packed with a lifetime of unique perspectives – wise insights into spiritual warfare, an infectious passion for revival and an overflowing heart of worship – I loved it.

Jeremy Simpkins
Team Leader, ChristCentral Churches (part of Newfrontiers)

David Fellingham has been a huge gift to the body of Christ in nearly fifty years of ministry. His blend of gifting as a pastor-teacher, a prophet and a worship leader especially equips him to unpack the book of Revelation. This is a book that will help many to see Jesus, to worship him, to pray, to believe God to fulfil his great purposes in the nations and to live a life of faithful witness in an increasingly dark world.

Andy Johnston
Senior Pastor, King's Community Church, Southampton

You may think that after being a Christian for more than forty years, including twenty in some form of leadership, and the last ten leading the eldership team at LIFESPRING, that the book of Revelation would have been removed from my 'too difficult' file. However, that changed when I read it alongside *The Unveiling*. It addressed many of my questions, debunked many myths and wrong teachings that perplexed me. Dave is a dear friend and someone I admire as a Bible teacher. This book is a fantastic study guide, and as the title suggests, unveils the truths hidden for us in John's incredible prophetic vision. It will equip and prepare the church for all that will happen between the ascension and the second coming, and prepare us to be the radiant bride, with a future hope. I thoroughly recommend *The Unveiling* and encourage you to take the book of Revelation out of the 'too difficult' file.

Andy Robinson is the lead elder of LIFESPRING in Horsham West Sussex, where Dave and Rosie Fellingham play an active part.

DEDICATION AND THANKS

To my wonderful wife Rosie, who has constantly supported and encouraged me throughout my life and ministry.

To my two sons and their wives, Luke and Rachel, Nathan and Louise, who continue to maintain the ministry through the generations.

To my six grandchildren Lucy, Poppy, Audrey, Jesse, Ella and Jude to whom I want to leave a kingdom legacy.

Special thanks to Andy Robinson who has supported and encouraged my ministry and helped make my latter years abundantly fruitful.

Thanks also to my LIFESPRING family in Horsham who have always been encouraging of my ministry.

ACKNOWLEDGEMENTS

This book is an introduction to the Book of Revelation. It is not a detailed study but outlines the main themes and opens the way for further study.

I have read many books and heard many talks on Revelation, but I have been particularly influenced by G.K. Beale's commentary. I have quoted him frequently and found his writings to be sound, not only theologically, but also logical, intellectually stimulating and, in particular, faith-building.

I am also very grateful to my good friend Dr David Campbell, who worked with G.K. Beale on an abridged version of his monumental work. David Campbell has helped to make Beale's work more accessible to people who do not have an academic background. He has also been helpful to me, giving me access to some personal notes which have helped to bring clarity to my thinking.

I know my book raises some questions and makes some assumptions whose development lie outside the scope of this book. I would therefore recommend that if further study is needed, use this book in conjunction with the shorter commentary by G.K. Beale with David Campbell.

My intention with *The Unveiling* is to connect with our everyday world and to see the relevance of the Book of Revelation to that context.

It is my prayer that it will inspire faith, expectation and motivation for world mission.

FOREWORD

At times, when major world events, like the current global pandemic, disturb our complacency, questions are often asked about whether these world events are specifically sent by God in judgement and/or are signs of the final days before the return of Jesus Christ.

Often well-meaning Christians can then turn to speculations about when the second coming will occur. This is in clear contravention of Jesus's reply to his apostles namely that 'it is not for you to know times or seasons that the Father has fixed by his own authority' (Acts 1:7 ESV). Rather their focus, and therefore ours today, was to be upon the mission of the church in the power of the Holy Spirit to preach the gospel all over the world.

My good friend, David Fellingham, has sought to answer many of these questions that arise by focusing us on the big picture of the lordship of Jesus over history (he 'is worthy to open the scroll') as revealed in the Book of Revelation, 'the Unveiling' of what is really going on from God's perspective throughout history.

The Book of Revelation was written to a church suffering persecution to assure them that God's sovereign purpose will be accomplished. Again, this is very relevant today. Although it is receiving fewer headlines than the pandemic, persecution against Christians across the world is greater now than at almost any other time in history.

Sometimes speculation about the details of the Book of Revelation have obscured rather than revealed the picture of the victory of Christ as has the way the term 'apocalypse' is used in popular literature and film. However, David Fellingham in *The Unveiling* continues his gift for clear teaching of the Word of God, with his evident passion for worship and experience as a worship leader. After all, the whole of the Book of Revelation is intended to lead us to worship the 'Lion who is also the Lamb' and to be confident regarding the accomplishment of God's purpose in mission resulting in a church formed of every ethnicity and language. David also draws from pastoral leadership experience in commenting upon the spiritual warfare dimension which is also part of the teaching of the Book of Revelation.

Reading *The Unveiling* reminded me of my first encounter with David Fellingham. He was preaching at a church, in the early 1980s, not far from where we live. My wife and I were in the process of exploring what was then called the 'charismatic renewal'. All I remember of David from that event was thorough biblical teaching, which impressed me, and tremendous skill on the trumpet!

The Unveiling combines helpful exposition on the Book of Revelation, avoiding unnecessary speculation, combined with a trumpet call to worship the God who reigns and the victorious Lamb of God:

'To him who sits on the throne and to the Lamb be blessing and honour and glory and might for ever and ever!' (Revelation 5:13 ESV)

David Devenish
Newfrontiers Together Team

PREFACE

When the Coronavirus first impacted the world, many people were asking me such questions as: Does the Bible have anything to say about this? Is the pandemic God's judgment on a sinful world? Is it a sign that Jesus is returning?

For more than fifty years I have been involved in church leadership as a Bible teacher, pastor and worship leader. I have been engaged in both prophetic and evangelistic ministry.

I guess questions have been fired at me because I have lived through many phases of history, both in the world and in the church. I have had the joy of teaching God's word in churches and conferences in many nations and continents across the globe, and although I am officially retired from church leadership, retirement is not a word in my vocabulary or lifestyle.

This breadth of life experience has created a network of relationships across the world and it is a privilege that I am still asked questions such as these.

I have personally asked myself the same questions. I have wanted to see if through the crisis of this particular pandemic, at the time of writing, whether there is a prophetic thrust which God is bringing to the church.

From boyhood I have had a fascination with eschatology and after years of study I am still learning, yet I have not found answers to every detail of end-time teaching.

However, there are certain truths which to me are, theologically speaking, non-negotiable.

The 'last days' is the whole period between the resurrection and the Second Coming of Christ. The gospel of the kingdom will reach every nation. The church is the highest priority on God's agenda. Before Jesus returns there will be a powerful church, alive in the Holy

Spirit, consisting of people from every tribe, tongue and nation.

I also believe the world in its fallen state will display great wickedness and opposition to the plans and purposes of God.

The victorious outcome and triumph of King Jesus will be demonstrated for all to see when he returns.

It is the Book of Revelation that draws the prophetic purposes of God together, with over five hundred allusions from other parts of the Bible, and it is the Bible itself which interprets this amazing book, not world events.

However, we can understand the events that are happening in our world through the prophetic lens of Revelation, and as we do that, we can grow in our faith that even with such devastating events like wars, natural disasters and pandemics, God is totally in control. He has an unfolding plan. As we Christians cooperate with King Jesus in the power of the Holy Spirit, we will see the Father's plan fulfilled.

There have been many speculative prophecies, articles, social media posts and YouTube clips claiming all kinds of interpretations of the current situation.

The writing of this book, *The Unveiling*, brings a perspective to answer the questions I have been asked.

The answers are not speculative, but firmly rooted in Scripture.

I do not have the answer for every detail, and I do know there will be other opinions and views, but whatever view we may hold the certain fact is, Jesus is coming again.

CONTENTS

CHAPTER 1
APOCALYPSE NOW

On 11 September 2001, my wife Rosie and I had just spent an incredible day exploring the ancient city of Ephesus. We were on holiday on the Greek island of Samos and were looking forward to a relaxed three-hour cruise back from mainland Turkey to where we were staying. As we cruised into the harbour at Samos, we could see a lot of activity on the quayside, with a strong police and military presence. There seemed to be a lot of agitation and when we were not allowed to dock, we sensed there was some sort of trouble. But we could not have imagined the terrible events that had happened just a few hours before, when two aeroplanes crashed into the twin towers in New York. After a wait of two hours, we were allowed to disembark and were herded out of the port and shipped onto the buses waiting to take us back to our accommodation.

Because of the remoteness of the apartment complex we were totally oblivious to what had been happening in America and why there was this sudden security clamp-down at a very quiet Greek island port.

It was not until the next day that news filtered through to us and of course, along with the rest of the world, our idyllic holiday was totally interrupted by the shocking news. In bars and restaurants, holiday makers from across Europe were buzzing with the devastating reports. The word 'Apocalypse' was on the tongues of many, regardless of the nation they were from.

It is a strange irony that the very next day we had another trip booked to the island of Patmos. We wondered if that trip might have been cancelled due to the frenetic activity at the port, but it went ahead. We were eagerly anticipating visiting the place where the apostle John wrote the Book of Revelation.

On our arrival, we were greeted by a guide who immediately started talking about these cataclysmic world events and relating them to the Apocalypse. She was very knowledgeable about the Book of Revelation and eager to visit the cave where it is believed John received his apocalyptic revelation. To hear her talking in such an animated fashion somehow made the relevance of the book come alive.

It made us ask the question: Is John's vision happening now? Are we experiencing the Apocalypse? It was a poignant and memorable visit. Since then we have been living in a more unstable world which seems to lurch from one tumultuous situation to another.

My parents lived through two World Wars after experiencing the economic disaster of the Great Depression through their early adulthood. My mother grew up in South Wales in the mining village where the 1904 revival broke out. The family home was close to where Welsh Revival figure Evan Roberts lived, near the marshes of the River Loughor estuary. The Industrial Revolution of the previous century had now settled into the economic structure of the UK. Urban industrial areas like South Wales were dependent on the work provided by the steel and coal industry. People worked hard and made enough to live.

In 1929 an economic collapse ushered in what was called the Great Depression. My grandfather lost his job in the steel works and for nine hard years he was unemployed. Money was scarce and life was hard. Ten years later, the Second World War broke out. When it ended, I was born.

I have lived through and remember most of the main events that have dominated the news and brought a sense of instability to the world.

Just five years after the end of the Second World War, 100,000 British troops were sent to the Far East to fight with the Americans against the North Koreans who had invaded South Korea. This is often referred to as the 'forgotten war'.

Many veterans of the Second World War dreaded being called up and the British fighting force was largely made up of new recruits who had been conscripted through the call-up to do National Service. Three years after the Korean War ended, the news was dominated by the Suez Crisis, and again it looked as though British troops would be sent to the Middle East. I can remember the uncertainty felt by members of my family who had fought in the Second World War. Would they be called up again to go and fight?

In the next decade, the Sixties, there was the growing crisis of the Cold War. The stand-off between the US and Russia over the Cuban missile crisis brought the whole world to the brink of nuclear war.

But it was not only the threat of wars and rumours of wars that hung over the planet. There were many other major social upheavals.

In the US, the Civil Rights movement led by the charismatic black leader Martin Luther King, gained incredible momentum as racism was exposed in the American social structure. His assassination in 1968 highlighted the problem on the world stage.

The evils of racism were also highlighted by the political system in South Africa with its apartheid policy. It came to the forefront of attention in Britain when there was a scheduled cricket tour of the MCC in 1968. Basil D'Oliveira was a brilliant test batsman but he was born in South Africa and labelled a 'Cape coloured'. This would mean that because of the apartheid laws he would not be allowed to tour with the English team in South Africa. After pressure from the South African government the English test selection committee omitted D'Oliveira's name from the touring party. It caused a major upset in the country with even non-cricket fans becoming outraged at this racist decision. The decision by the MCC was overturned when Tom Cartwright withdrew from the team because of injury. D'Oliveira was now included but this was unacceptable to the South African government. The tour was called off and this isolated South Africa from international sport until apartheid was dismantled. Although there was outrage at this blatant racism, in England there was still an underbelly of racial prejudice.

The late Sixties saw an influx of immigrants from Commonwealth countries and Enoch Powell, a conservative MP in Edward Heath's shadow cabinet, made an anti-immigration speech where he suggested that the end result of the influx of immigrants would be akin to the River Tiber flowing with blood. It became known as the 'river of blood' speech. Although he was dismissed from the shadow cabinet it is generally thought that the popularity of this speech helped the Conservatives win the next election. If that is true, it is chilling.

By the Seventies there was incredible social unrest caused by the miners' strike. This divided communities and it also brought about the three-day week.

The Eighties and Nineties brought rumblings and protests about a whole number of social issues which caused divisions in society. Two wars in Iraq gave rise to many anti-war demonstrations and the presence of troops in Afghanistan also came into question. The HIV crisis which entered public awareness during the Eighties became a focal point of attention in the world news in the early Nineties. It was estimated that between eight and ten million people worldwide might be infected.

In recent years, other major diseases have emerged like SARS and this year (2020) the Coronavirus pandemic has dominated world news.

The debates and discussions over Brexit have also brought yet more uncertainty, polarising and dividing the nation.

The world is bigger than Britain and Europe and the unrest in places like Hong Kong, India and Pakistan show that the issues that trouble us are global. The whole of humanity is affected.

It is almost on a daily basis that there are news reports of tensions in the Middle East. It seems to be a cauldron of conflict, ready to spill over at any moment. The issues are complex, and one crisis may not necessarily be related to another. There is a long history of strained relationships dating back to the years between the eleventh and thirteenth centuries.

The political and religious obstacles between Christians (using this name as a political, rather than a faith definition), Jews and Muslims, has dominated world politics in the Common Era. Words like 'crusade' and the Arabic word 'jihad' have created tensions and conflict

The Middle East became a theatre of activity in the two world wars of the twentieth century. The aftermath of political decisions made in 1917 with the Balfour Declaration, and the establishment of Israel as a nation in 1948, have created ongoing tensions. The cauldron is constantly seething and spilling over, threatening world peace.

The civil war in Syria, which has the superpowers looking on and if necessary ready to act, is regularly on our news channels. The heartbreaking sight of countless refugees, the genocide of the Kurds, and the nuclear threat with Iran, show that we live in an unstable world.

We have also had to live through economic uncertainties, such as the financial collapse in 2008. The economic prospects post coronavirus make many fearful about the future.

In addition to all this, the ecological challenges to the planet and climate change combine to create a depressingly unstable outlook for the future.

What hope is there for humanity? Are we evolving into a more tolerant, peaceful, loving world or will we continue as we are, making the same mistakes, experiencing the same tensions, living with the same fears?

Will the world eventually evolve into a non-combatant place where everyone loves each other, where nations co-operate, where family life is free from hurt and pain, where sickness and disease are eradicated, where everyone is valued regardless of their ethnicity and where hurt and pain, wars and strife are eradicated? Will there be a time when music and the arts are valued and enjoyed, when the wealth creators of a country share their efforts to help eradicate poverty?

This dream has been expressed in all kinds of movements and it has been explored, particularly in the world of pop music.

In the mid-Sixties, protests about race, armaments, equality and social justice were gaining in prominence, especially amongst the 'baby boomer' generation. There were many pop artists who articulated their message, giving that generation anthems to feed their radicalism (as it was seen to be then by a previous generation).

A seminal song from that era was 'Last Night I Had the Strangest Dream.' The lyrics of this song, written by a small-time American singer, Ed McMurdy, expressed the dream of a day when there would be a gathering of men, peace treaties signed, guns and uniforms surrendered and a world agreement never to fight again. The song ends with a vision of humanity rejoicing over the ending of war, and a vow never to fight again. The folk singer Joan Baez popularized it in the folk clubs, gathering places for the younger generation of that time. It was the recording by Simon and Garfunkel that brought this song to the attention of mainstream pop music. It permeated deep into the psyche of a generation and fuelled protests about the war in Vietnam, bringing an optimistic hope for a more peaceful future.

The early Sixties were a time of social turbulence especially among the teenage generation, who, through the influence of their music, began to abandon the values of their parents. Bob Dylan's two songs, 'Blowin' in the Wind' and 'The Times They Are A-Changin'', articulated the changing values of a generation looking for a new, more peaceful world.

The impact of the Beatles and the cultural revolution that came about through their popularity, is now well documented as a sociological phenomenon.

By the end of the Sixties, the Beatles had transitioned from the zany, fun-loving days of 'A Hard Day's Night' to a highly influential voice creating a greater liberation in attitudes to sex and drugs. They also highlighted the anti-war message.

In 1969 John Lennon wrote and recorded 'Give Peace a Chance', followed in 1972 by the Christmas hit, 'Merry Xmas (War is Over)', with the ever-hopeful thought that war is over if we want it. This is still played as a Christmas classic.

Although the 'peace movement' gained momentum, with many of these songs as their anthems, sadly the world has continued with yet more conflict between nations.

The pop music and film industries are speaking into current social issues. Films like the highly acclaimed *Green Book* and anthemic songs, like 'What About Us' by Pink are just two examples of the music and film industries highlighting social issues.

The graphic images on TV news and heart-rending advertisements from a multiplicity of charities show that there is incredible pain in the world but there do not seem to be any solutions.

Whatever the rights and wrongs of the Falklands War, the two wars in Iraq, and the conflicts in Afghanistan and the Middle East, we are well into the twenty-first century facing the same problems of conflict in humanity. The heart-breaking sight on our TV screens of thousands of refugees from places like Syria betrays the sad fact that the human race has not changed very much.

The dream still lives for a better, fairer, more compassionate world. Will that ever be possible?

Not only is the world of human relationships complex, there are ecological issues which are manmade and in the natural world such disasters as earthquakes, tsunamis, strange weather patterns causing flooding, fires, and other devastations such as crumbling cliffs that can bring about insecurities and fears regarding the future. The question of racial tension has again reared its ugly head with the murder of George Floyd in Minneapolis. It has brought the Black Lives Matter campaign to the forefront of world news and created civil unrest in cities across the world.

A white, Western, American-European populace has tended to think of history on their terms. Even within the church, people forget that such Christian theologians as Augustine of Hippo, Tertullian and Athanasius were African and by the second century the African church was incredibly influential. Augustine had a profound influence upon Luther and Calvin and thus upon the Reformation. The Book of Revelation frequently refers to every tribe, tongue and nation.

Church history and its place in world history is not just about Europe and America but about the whole earth.

Although I have highlighted some of the key points in Western, white history, other nations have had their histories, their dramas, their cataclysmic events, their wars, their sufferings, their injustices. God is sovereign over every nation.

It is in the Bible that we find answers to these issues, but they are not simplistic or naïve. The Bible unfolds God's plan for the world and the human race, and it is in the Book of Revelation that the vision for a better world and the eternal fate of the human race is unveiled. Some of it may be uncomfortable to face, but if we can unravel what this amazing book is saying it will help us to understand the world in which we live and what its future will be.

We tend to think of 'Apocalypse' as an 'end of the world' type of word. It is associated with climactic and foreboding events. The

Greek word 'apokalupsis' means to uncover, to reveal. The final book of the Bible is an 'apokalupsis', a revelation, a revealing of God's plan throughout history. It's a plan for the church and the world. Although we do read about the final days on Planet Earth, the bigger theme revealed is that God has been sovereign over the whole history of the world. He has a plan from the beginning to the end of the world as we know it. The 'apocalypse' is happening now and has been throughout history.

It is the Book of Revelation that holds the keys to help us understand our world now and our future.

CHAPTER 2
VISIONS, SYMBOLS, INTERPRETATION
Read Revelation 1

The Book of Revelation, along with Genesis, is probably the most controversial book in the Bible. If we are going to understand its message it is important that we approach it in the correct way.

I first became interested in this book over sixty years ago when my parents took me as a fifteen-year-old boy to hear a well-known preacher from that era. He was a Major in the Salvation Army and he was very much a 'blood and fire' Salvationist. He was an outstanding preacher and his ministry reached well beyond the Army. He was a favourite at the Keswick Convention and was very strong on being filled with the Holy Spirit. In 1960, before the charismatic movement, anyone hungry for God would drive miles to hear anyone preaching about the Holy Spirit. My parents felt it would be good for me to hear this man and that day I was inspired to follow God wholeheartedly. I was shocked as Major Alistair Smith preached on the Second Coming and said that there was every possibility that Jesus could return within the next forty years. This created in me a hunger to find out more, to search the Scriptures and make sure I was ready. Sixty years on I still have the same urgency and excitement I had as a fifteen-year-old but as the years have gone by, and after much study and around fifty years in ministry, I have come to conclusions that have shaped what I now believe.

At that time, in the evangelical world I was in, the prevailing idea in the theology of the end times was dispensational pre-millennialism. (We will look at this in more depth when we eventually get to Revelation chapter 20 and we discuss the millennium.) This was a system of interpreting Scripture promoted by an Irish Anglican, J.N.

Darby, who became a founding leader of the Plymouth Brethren. The Scofield Reference Bible with its detailed notes became the textbook for a system of belief that indicated that the history of the world had been divided up into different dispensations. It places a strong emphasis on the Jewish nation, especially in the end times. It is a very complex system of belief with charts, maps and countless fanciful ideas about Bible prophecy.

However, within the system, there were different interpretations regarding the details of the end times. The main themes were that Israel would go back to its original land, there would be a time of great tribulation on the earth with other world powers 'ganging up' on Israel, the church would be generally weak and lukewarm and Jesus would suddenly come and 'rapture' the faithful.

There would be seven years of terrible tribulation from which the true church would escape. However, there were some adherents to this belief system who thought the church would have to endure three and a half years of the tribulation and that the rapture would take place halfway through. In this system Jesus seems to come again at least twice, first of all before or during the tribulation and then at the end of it to establish a kingdom on earth for a thousand years, during which Jesus reigns from Jerusalem, with Israel right at the centre of government.

This view was popular amongst many evangelicals and when the Pentecostal movement began in the early twentieth century they also took this teaching on board. It is a complex system of teaching and not within the remit of this study to develop it.

The popularity of this view was captured in the rise of the Christian music scene in the late Sixties with the hugely popular song 'I Wish We'd All Been Ready' by Larry Norman. The idea of a rapture with people being taken and others left was the prevailing thought.

The book *Late Great Planet Earth* by Hal Lindsey, which was published in 1970, proved to be one of the most widely read Christian books at that time and fully endorsed the teachings of Darby.

Although this particular eschatological or end-times view has been adopted by many evangelicals, Pentecostals and charismatics, other significant mainline Evangelical theologians have challenged it.

Our salvation is not dependent on our particular view of eschatology, so it is very important not to allow dogma to cause division and disunity. Christian love must be at the heart of everything we believe. However, it is important to apply principles of biblical interpretation and exegesis to all Scripture and we need to do this carefully as we approach the Book of Revelation. Our understanding of this book will help us to know what we believe about God, our salvation, the church, our eternal destiny and whether our life is motivated by fear or faith .

There are four main views regarding the interpretation of Revelation but even within these views there can be areas of difference. Here is a simplified definition of each view:

1. The PRETERIST view believes that the Matthew 24 Olivet discourse and the Book of Revelation have been fulfilled already in the events surrounding the fall of Jerusalem in AD 70. This was a devastating and cataclysmic event for the Jewish people and launched the next 2,000 years of their history. The Roman armies, under the leadership of the Roman commander Titus, besieged and destroyed the city and reduced the Temple to rubble. Jesus had prophesied that this would happen and preterists believe that these events fulfil the prophecy of Matthew 24 and the Book of Revelation.

2. The HISTORICIST view sees the letters to the seven churches and the visions in chronological order. The seven churches and the outpourings of the judgments represent consecutive ages in church history. The problem with this view is that it is difficult to ascertain which parts of Revelation can be identified with particular events.

3. The FUTURIST view sees everything in the Book of Revelation from Revelation chapter 4 to 19 relating to the events in the period immediately before Christ's return. Futurists believe that the Jewish people are restored to Israel and the church is secretly raptured into heaven. There will be plagues, the appearance of the Antichrist, a seven-year tribulation, a thousand-year reign of Christ on the earth, a rebuilt Temple, a final war and then Jesus comes again, again! This view is the exact opposite to the preterist view.

4. The IDEALIST view sees the book as a symbolic and prophetic message to prepare the church for its on-going battle with the world and the devil from the time of Jesus's resurrection to the time he comes again. It is not to be taken chronologically but the letters and the visions are parallel perspectives, each one developing in intensity to show that the church will go through trials and tribulations but will always be victorious. It will end when Jesus returns, and the future will be in the new heaven and earth.

It is the Idealist view from which the rest of my teaching will come. G.K. Beale[1] in his commentary calls this the CONTEMPORARY RELEVANCE VIEW. I have combined the thought between these two titles and called it THE REDEMPTIVE HISTORICAL IDEALIST VIEW.

If these different views exist, how do we know which is the right one? Is it even possible to find a definitive view that will answer every question? Will my conclusions about this affect my love for Jesus, other Christians, my faith?

It is important not to be dogmatic, but it is vital that we apply correct principles for interpreting Scripture and as we do so that we ask God to speak by his Spirit. The approach I am taking is after many years of study, asking questions, looking at church history, looking at world history and drawing conclusions that are both spiritually and intellectually satisfying.

When we read the Bible, we must understand the particular passage we are reading. Is it narrative? Is it prophecy? Is it history? Is it poetry? Is it theological teaching? Is it a letter and if so, to whom was it written and why? All of these questions help us to understand not just what the words say but the context and what meaning is to be conveyed. Of course, the Bible is God-breathed, totally inspired by the Holy Spirit. We must approach it in that way but also apply our minds to understand literary principles so we can understand what the writer intended. In his book *How to Read the Bible for All Its Worth*, Gordon Fee says in the chapter on Revelation:

'The first task of the exegesis of Revelation is to seek the author's, and there with the Holy Spirit's, original intent. As with the epistles, the primary meaning of the Revelation is what John intended it to mean, which in turn must have been something his readers could have understood it to mean.'[2]

It would be wrong to interpret the Book of Revelation through contemporary world events. There have been many fanciful interpretations from seeing the European Union prophesied, to helicopter warfare! Revelation has more references to other books in the Bible than any other book. There are over 500 allusions which give us some clues as to how the book should be interpreted. The Bible interprets itself and the context of those references and allusions will give us insight as to how we understand John's vision.

Revelation is apocalyptic literature and thus has to be read in that way. John's original readers would have been familiar with many pieces of apocalyptic literature. They would have understood that the visions and symbols were never meant to be taken literally. A number of Old Testament books are also apocalyptic and again John's readers would have been familiar with such books as Daniel, Ezekiel and Zechariah, all of which are referenced in Revelation.

CHAPTER 3
PROLOGUE TO THE VISION
Read Revelation 1

In the first verse we get an important clue as to how this book should be interpreted.

Revelation 1:1 says: 'The Revelation of Jesus Christ, which God gave Him to show His servants – things which must shortly take place. And He sent and signified [Greek word *'semaino'*] it by His angel to His servant John' (NKJV).

The Greek word *'semaino'* is important and it is only the NKJV that translates it accurately. The NASB translates it 'communicated' but has 'signified' as an alternative in the margin. The NIV and the ESV have translated it 'made it known' and the NLT has translated it 'present'.

In his commentary, G.K. Beale argues that the use of the word *'semaino'* 'suggests a symbolic communication and not mere conveyance of information. Therefore, John's use of *"semaino"* rather than *"gnorizo"* (make known) is not haphazard but intentional. It is associated with Daniel 2:45, an apocalyptic passage of which John would have been aware. John deliberately uses the language of *"signify"* from Daniel in part to portray that which God has been showing him.'[3]

In Kittel's *Theological Dictionary of the New Testament* he says that the root word from which *'semaino'* is derived, *'semeion'*, is used for all kinds of symbolism, optical impressions, acoustic omens (like thunder), symbols and prophetic actions.[4] (This is an abridged summary.)

There can therefore be no logical reason to take the Book of Revelation literally. It is a symbolic book conveying God's will and purpose and we cannot arbitrarily choose which parts are literal and which are symbolic. We must be consistent in the way we interpret John's vision.

The symbolism of Revelation can be grouped in four main categories:

1. There are material objects: lampstands, thrones, crowns, the sea, the wind.
2. There are symbolic numbers: the number seven is a symbol of completion and perfection. The number four speaks of the whole earth. Six is the number of man and the number twelve and its multiples signify the people of God.
3. There are creatures which could have come straight out of a fantasy movie – dragons, serpents, the beast, horses with the heads of lions, locusts with the faces of men and living creatures full of eyes.
4. Finally there is the symbolism of time. There are periods of time mentioned that can mislead the literalists. The millennium, a period of one thousand years; numbers of days like three and a half years; silence in heaven for half an hour. These are all symbolic.

Much of the symbolism is rooted in the Old Testament and as the vision unfolds, the significance of the numbers, the creatures, the objects and the time become clearer.

The Godhead is represented symbolically by the fact that the name of Christ appears seven times, Jesus and the Spirit fourteen times and the Lamb twenty-eight times.[5]

The Book of Revelation is actually a pastoral letter to the seven churches and so it is relevant to today's church because it raises issues which are always with us. It is also a prophetic message equipping the church to face trials and difficulties but bringing assurance of eternal destiny.

Having introduced the way in which we should interpret the vision, the prologue continues with a blessing upon those who pay attention to this prophecy.

The blessing comes upon those who read, hear and keep it and Revelation 1:3 says the words 'for the time is near'. This shows the immediacy of the message and relates to the fact that the last days are the whole period between the resurrection and the Second Coming. In the New Testament there are several references to the last days from this perspective. It is only the closing chapters of Revelation that deal with the final day of the last days.

THE TRINITARIAN MESSAGE OF REVELATION

After the prologue John addresses the seven churches as though God himself is speaking to them and we see the Father, the Holy Spirit and the Son together and as one conveying the message. Revelation 1 is one of the great Trinitarian passages in the New Testament. God is described as him 'who is and who was and who is to come'.[6] This theme recurs through the book, showing God to be the eternal God. The seven spirits before the throne are the one Holy Spirit, the number seven speaking of his fullness and when we come into the throne room in chapter four, we will consider this in more depth. Jesus Christ is called the 'faithful witness, the firstborn from the dead'.[7] The word here for 'firstborn' is 'prototokos' and Paul uses the same word and concept in Colossians 1:15. The phrase 'firstborn from the dead' has been misinterpreted by the Jehovah's Witnesses who believe that God created Jesus Christ because of the expression 'firstborn'. What this actually means is that Jesus through his resurrection is the first of this new species of human beings who have been raised through his death and resurrection. His resurrection becomes ours. The resurrection shows Jesus's supreme rank over the created world. The Old Testament viewed the resurrection of physical bodies as an end-time event signalling the coming of God's eternal kingdom. Douglas Moo in his commentary on Colossians says:

'Jesus's resurrection initiates this end time resurrection; his resurrection guarantees, indeed stimulates the resurrection of all who follow. Jesus is not only the first one to experience Resurrection, he is the founder of the new order of resurrection – the firstborn ('*prototokos*'), of many brothers and sisters. The expression 'firstborn' is not referring to chronology, but supremacy.'[8]

Before Jesus's resurrection there were others in the Bible who had been raised from the dead, even in the Old Testament. In the gospels there were three people Jesus raised from the dead: Jairus' daughter, the widow of Nain's son and Lazarus. However, they all died again. They were not resurrected in the sense that Jesus was.

I have witnessed someone being raised from the dead. It happened in a large church where I had just preached on Whit Sunday, encouraging people to believe that the experience of the disciples on the day of Pentecost was available for us today. I also claimed that the signs and wonders that followed Jesus were also available for the contemporary church. At the end of the sermon when I was shaking hands with everyone in a very crowded vestibule as they were leaving the service, to my horror a man collapsed and his heart stopped. I had just preached on the ministry of the miraculous. I felt very vulnerable and exposed. The senior church warden was standing nearby. He was a well-known consultant at the local hospital, and he was also very sceptical about the ministry of the Holy Spirit and healing.

The doctor went immediately to the man and administered resuscitation principles, performing mouth to mouth and pummelling the heart, but without response. This was in the days before mobile phones and it was some time before someone could get to a telephone box to call the ambulance. By now several minutes had gone by and the man was clearly lifeless. I asked the doctor if he would mind me praying, not actually being sure of what I would pray for. He agreed and so I knelt down beside the man, laid my hands on him and prayed that he would have life. It was a speculative prayer rather than faith-filled, and life could have meant eternal life. After a few moments the man sat bolt upright and began to breathe. Very soon the ambulance arrived and took him to hospital. The man had come to church on his own and nobody seemed to know him. My wife's father agreed to accompany him to the hospital. Later that evening my father-in-law led this man to the Lord. He was not a Christian, but that night he was saved. Very much later that night the sceptical doctor called me and said that he had witnessed a miracle. As far as he was concerned, the man had died and now he was alive. Over the next few weeks my father-in-law looked after him and discipled him. Six months later the man died, but he died knowing Jesus. The doctor and I became great friends. His scepticism about the miraculous disappeared.

The point of this story, for which I fully give God the glory, is that even where there have been raisings from the dead people will eventually die, but Jesus, the '*prototokos*' was not only raised, he is forever risen, the first of a whole new race who will share in his resurrection. I love the Latin word '*resurgam*'. It means 'I shall rise'. Revelation 1 shows Jesus in all his risen glory. The promise is that he will return once 'the Lamb for sinners slain' but now seen as the Alpha and Omega, the beginning and the end. We have the description again of God as the one who was and is and is to come.

John sees him as God Almighty, 'pantokrator'. There is no other word in Greek that can describe the great, omnipotent, invincible God.

We also get this marvellous statement about the people of God, the church who are described as a loved people, who have been set free from sin by the blood of Jesus and now made to be a kingdom of priests thus fulfilling God's original intention for his people.

In Exodus, after the deliverance from Egypt, God gave the people and Moses a promise: 'If you will indeed obey my voice and keep my covenant, you shall be my treasured possession among all the peoples, for all the earth is mine; and you shall be to me a kingdom of priests and a holy nation' (Exodus 19:5-6 ESV).

At first, the people went along with this great promise which they thought would be a recovery of the priesthood and rulership that Adam had enjoyed before the fall, but it was not to be. Sin and rebellion meant that the people refused to live in the good of this promise. The rest of the Old Testament is a record of one disaster after another as God's people were constantly rebelling against him. But here in Revelation, the second Adam who came as the perfect prophet, priest and king, has purchased a people with his blood. The church is drawn from every tribe, tongue and nation as a people who fulfil God's original intention. The church is not about one nation Israel but about this multitude. This is a theme running through the whole apocalyptic vision.

Having established that, this letter to the seven churches is from God who has revealed himself as Father, Son and Spirit. John outlines how he received the vision. He says he was 'in the Spirit on the Lord's Day'.[9] The right posture to receive from God is to be 'in the Spirit'. That must mean he was yielded to and fellowshipping with the Holy Spirit. It is the Holy Spirit who brings the reality of God's presence to us. When we are fully yielded to him, he will speak. John would have also been filled with the word of God. He starts to hear a voice and see a vision. This vision is redolent of the visions of Ezekiel and Zechariah as he sees the golden lampstands. It is important that any vision or prophetic word we may have is rooted in both the Spirit and the Word.

It is then that we have one of the most powerful descriptions of the risen, ascended Christ in all his majesty and glory.

John sees Jesus as one 'like a son of man' (Revelation 1:13). He is clothed with a long robe with a golden sash around his chest. This speaks of his priesthood. He is our great High Priest, ever living to intercede for us, empathizing with us, feeling our pain and weakness, having gone through every human trial imaginable. Here he is now glorified at the right hand of the Father.

The hairs of his head were white like wool, like snow, speaking of his absolute purity and maturity and identifying him with the Ancient of Days in the vision of Daniel and revealing Jesus to be the God of the Old Testament. His eyes were like a flaming fire, penetrating, all-seeing. His feet were like burnished bronze, his voice like the roar of many waters. In his hand he was holding seven stars representing the seven churches and from his mouth came a sharp two-edged sword. Jesus, the Word made flesh in his appearance on earth is now in his glorified state, his word still powerful and penetrating. The ultimate truth!

His face was like the sun shining in its full strength. The awesomeness of the vision overwhelms John who falls at his feet as though he were dead. But fear gives way to faith as Jesus speaks words of reassurance. It is Jesus who holds the keys of Hades and Death. It is reassuring that he knows the number of our days and a great comfort to the bereaved, even when death is premature. Here is the Lord of Glory, the great I Am, the Sovereign King of the heavens and the earth who has borne the pain of the sins of the world and who completely conquered death. He is the one who is about to unfold the mysteries and secrets of the world and its future to the disciple who, as a younger man, leaned on his breast, and in human terms was much loved.

The first and the last, the one who is alive forevermore, commands John to write down what he is about to see.

It is impossible to read this passage and not be filled with worship. In the early Eighties the Holy Spirit was restoring worship to the church and was raising up a new generation of songwriters who were giving expression to all that God was doing at that time. One day as I sat at my piano, I began to read aloud this description of Jesus. As I was reading my hands began to move over the keys and I began to sing. The words, melody and harmony were instantaneous. The song has now gone all over the world.

AT YOUR FEET WE FALL

At your feet we fall, mighty risen Lord,
As we come before your throne to worship you.
By your Spirit's power, you now draw our hearts,
And we hear your voice in triumph ringing clear.

I am he that liveth, that liveth and was dead.
Behold I am alive for evermore.

There we see you stand, mighty risen Lord,
Clothed in garments pure and holy shining bright.
Eyes of flashing fire, feet like burnished bronze.
And the sound of many waters is your voice.

Like the shining sun, in its noon day strength,
We now see the glories of your wondrous face.

Once that face was marred, but now you're glorified
And your words like a two-edged sword have mighty power.
(Copyright © 1982 Thankyou Music)[10]

One of the most profound experiences of my life was to join with a number of people in the Garden Tomb in Jerusalem and sing this song, celebrating the glories of the risen Lord Jesus in the actual place where the resurrection is believed to have taken place. For me the reality of his presence is as great today as ever! It was, when I wrote the song, when I sang it at the Garden Tomb, and it is every moment of every day.

CHAPTER 4
WELCOME TO THE CHURCH
Read Revelation 2 and 3

When speaking with people who are not Christians and trying to share my faith with them, their perception of church is a frequent stumbling block. They may well affirm the teachings of Jesus but express all kinds of opinions ranging from accusations of hypocrisy to it being an anachronism in today's world. Perceptions of outdated language and music to 'they're only after your money' all add to the mix. The media does not help, often reporting that churches are empty, and that church attendance has dwindled to almost nothing. Occasionally a spokesperson for the church may be interviewed on the TV news to get their opinion on some current topic or event, but the choice of person interviewed is often someone dressed in clerical dress and they appear to be irrelevant.

The problem is exacerbated by the fact that so many denominations and church groupings appear to be fractured and disunited. The first session of the Alpha course deals with the issue of 'Christianity: Boring, Untrue and Irrelevant'. Nicky Gumbel, the founder of the Alpha course, is certainly in touch with the perceptions of most people as he tackles this subject.

Denominationalism and party spirit have been a huge problem throughout church history and splits from denominations, usually over such issues as doctrine and church government, have littered two thousand years of history.

In 1054 the split between the Catholic Church and the Eastern Orthodox churches became known as the 'great schism'.

In the sixteenth century the Reformation created a huge divide between the Catholic Church and Protestants, with each group often identifying with political and nationalistic ideologies, which brought not only ecclesiastical divisions, but tensions between nations.

Many broke away from what might be termed the ecclesiastical establishment, and many non-conformist churches were formed, seeking a purer, more biblical expression of church.

At the beginning of the twentieth century, the Pentecostal movement emphasised the ministry of the Holy Spirit with a renewal of such gifts as speaking in tongues, prophecy and healing.

During the first half of the twentieth century, the Pentecostals were regarded with great suspicion by the evangelical world.

In the late Sixties there was a move of the Holy Spirit that saw several traditional evangelical churches, alongside some Catholics, experience some of the phenomena that made the Pentecostals distinctive.

The charismatic movement polarised the evangelical world, creating yet more division.

It is no wonder non-Christians are confused.

I have had first-hand experience of four denominations. I was brought up in the Salvation Army. My grandfather was an officer in the days of William Booth and saw scenes of revival and was a great soulwinner. My parents were Salvation Army officers when I was born. My wife Rosie was in the Pentecostal Church when we met and we both experienced prejudice from both sides. After our marriage we were part of the Elim Church. When God called me out of my job as a director of music in a high school it was to join the staff of a vibrant evangelical Anglican church. However, I caught the vision to see the church restored to a more biblical structure and became what was known in the late Seventies as a 'Restorationist'. Over the past forty years, it has been my passion to see the church restored to a more biblical structure, with the dynamic of New Testament church life empowered by the Holy Spirit.

In the UK there is a much greater unity today among evangelicals and charismatics and worship has been a big key in drawing people together. In the worldwide church there is a long way to go but Jesus said that he would build his church and that the gates of hell would not prevail against it. He also prayed that his people may be one. The Book of Revelation has a very high view of the church with a vision for its unity and central place in God's plans. God has always intended to have a people who would be his treasured possession, a people upon whom he would bestow all his affection, who would be cherished and nurtured and would fulfil his desire for the earth. The big Bible story is all about the people of God with the nation of Israel as the prototype of what was his ultimate desire, not just Israel, but a people from every tribe, tongue and nation. It was for this purpose that Jesus died, not just for our personal salvation but that corporately we might become the bride, the wife of the Lamb.

Ephesians 5:25-27 says: 'Christ also loved the church and gave Himself for her, that He might sanctify and cleanse her with the washing of water by the word, that He might present her to Himself a glorious church, not having spot or wrinkle or any such thing, but that she should be holy and without blemish' (NKJV).

The Book of Revelation unfolds that sanctifying process to show us that in spite of all her failings, the church is a priority on God's agenda, because the ultimate end is that she will be the bride of the Lamb.

This pastoral letter to the seven churches exposes some of the problems that have been mentioned throughout church history, to bring warnings of impending judgments so that the process of sanctifying and purifying the church can prepare her for her destiny. The seven churches represent the church in every age and the issues raised are totally relevant to today's church.

At the end of Revelation 1, before John sees the vision of Jesus, he sees another vision, one of seven golden lampstands. In Numbers 8, Moses commanded Aaron to make seven lamps for the tabernacle and John's vision connects with this. The lampstands were symbolic of God's presence. Later in the Temple the lampstands were placed for the same purpose.

In Zechariah's apocalyptic vision, where he prophesies about the coming Messianic Age, he sees a vision of a golden lampstand and two olive trees. It is in this vision that Zechariah says, as he prophesies about the future kingdom: '"Not by might nor by power, but by my Spirit," says the LORD Almighty' (Zechariah 4:6, NIV). This symbolism, repeated in Revelation, connects with what John is seeing.

The lampstands are the seven churches to whom John is writing.

The seven stars mentioned are the angelic representatives of the churches and the seven spirits are the eyes of God who sees everything and from whom no one can hide.

'Welcome to the church' can be said sarcastically if we have a negative view, but it can also be said with joyful anticipation that even as we identify its weaknesses, God is at work. The seven churches represent the church in every age.

EPHESUS (Revelation 2:1-7)

In Acts chapter 19 we read how the church in Ephesus was started by Paul. It soon grew into a thriving, dynamic church and eventually Timothy became the apostolic leader there. In the later years of his life John himself was there and apparently his constant message to that church was 'Little children, love one another'. This church is commended for its orthodoxy, zeal and standing against false doctrine. (The Nicolaitans were a cultic group who tried to influence the church.)

Beale sees these and the Balaam group, as linked with idolatrous practices which were infiltrating the seven churches in line with the initiation of Emperor worship.

This would have been the next generation from when Paul had founded the church in Ephesus and they were already beginning to compromise, abandoning their first love.

There is a warning to the church in every age that when there is a revival or a move of the Holy Spirit, the next generation often dilutes some of what the previous generation had pioneered. I once heard Church of England minister, Bible teacher and author Ian Barclay say that what begins as a movement can become a machine and end up as a monument.

SMYRNA (Revelation 2:8-11)

Christ commends the church in Smyrna (Izmir in modern-day Turkey) for enduring tribulation and encourages it to be faithful in anticipation of imminent and more severe persecution, in order to receive the crown of life (eternal reward). The persecution seems to be coming from the Jews who are called the 'synagogue of Satan'. The reference to ten days shows that their suffering would be limited.

The message was: Don't be fearful. Stay faithful.

PERGAMUM (Revelation 2:12-17)

Christ commends the church for its persevering witness in the midst of persecution but condemns it for its permissive spirit. Pergamum was a centre of idolatrous, occult spirituality. Satan's throne was said to be there.

The mention of Balaam and the Nicolaitans again speaks of spiritual compromise. In order to keep their jobs, church members might occasionally attend heathen festivals to keep the authorities at bay, thereby compromising their faith as a protection and security in the secular world.

There are many issues that challenge Christian beliefs and morals, and if believers go along with the stance typically adopted in the workplace, it may cause them to compromise their faith.

THYATIRA (Revelation 2:18-29)

The church is commended for its works of witness and endurance, but again we have a problem with compromise. Their tolerance of Jezebel is thoroughly condemned. How do we identify Jezebel?

In 1 Kings 16:29-34 we read how Ahab the king of Israel married Jezebel the daughter of the wicked king Ethbaal who ruled the Sidonians. This was in direct disobedience to God. Jezebel was a crusading Baal worshipper with all its occult practice, violence, sexual perversion and fertility rites. She manipulated both her husband and the political situation, constantly opposing the worship of Yahweh. She undermined the prophet Elijah and so intimidated him that even after he had won a great spiritual victory over the prophets of Baal on Mount Carmel, in a deep depression he became suicidal. Her end was violent and brutal. God would not allow this to continue.

Jezebel is a demonic spirit that seeks to destroy churches through compromise, manipulation and control of leadership, often creating tensions between the sexes. The Jezebel spirit will often use spiritual language, sometimes under the guise of the prophetic to work its evil intentions.

It is important to realize that both men and women can be affected by this and come under its control. The best way to deal with this is for churches to have a well-balanced understanding of how men and women complement each other, and leadership is operated through submissive, humble, serving hearts. Church life should create a healthy environment where men and women together can function fully in the gifting God has given them. There is no place for anything Jezebelic in church life and that is why it should not be tolerated. Over the years I have had the challenge and joy of helping churches work through issues such as these.

The letter to Thyatira gives an exhortation to overcome this. With victory over this issue there is a promise of released spiritual authority.

SARDIS (Revelation 3:1-6)

This was a church with a reputation but with no substance. It looks alive but is actually dead. The call is to wake up and revive truth because God could break in at any time. Yes, there are a few who are 'walking in white' but the call is for the church to repent. Having a name and a good reputation is not enough.

PHILADELPHIA (Revelation 3:7-13)

Philadelphia was founded by Attalus the Second who was loyal to his brother Fumenes, hence the name Philadelphia meaning 'brotherly love' – an appropriate name for a good church. This is yet another church that has to face the synagogue of Satan; opposition from the Jews. Jesus commends this church and it is a good example for us today, with some great promises. It is commended for its persevering witness and there is a promise that it will be strengthened even more, and that there will be an open door which no one can shut.

They are promised the key of David. In his earthly line Jesus is the royal son of David. The narrative of David's story, the establishing of the kingdom, the Messianic psalms, his prophetic anticipation of the nations worshipping and his desire to build a house for God are all fulfilled in the New Testament church.

This church is promised that it will be sustained, and that God's promises will be fulfilled. They will be given a name with the promise of the new Jerusalem.

LAODICEA (Revelation 3:14-22)

Christ condemns the church in Laodicea for its ineffective witness and deplorable spiritual condition. Its members are exhorted to persevere by becoming faithful witnesses and renewing their fellowship with him so as to reign with him. Earthly riches are not a sign of spiritual riches and their self-sufficiency is condemned. They are to be purified like gold in the fire. As Christ stands at the door knocking, they are to let him in. The inference is that they have shut Jesus out.

The famous reference to being neither hot nor cold but lukewarm can be very easily misunderstood. It is not that hot is good, cold is bad and lukewarm is mediocre. G.K. Beale in his commentary says:

'Laodicea had two neighbours Hierapolis and Colossae. Hierapolis had hot waters which possessed medicinal effects, while Colossae had cold water which was also thought to be healthy. Laodicea had no good water source, and water had to be piped in. By the time it arrived, it was lukewarm and dirty, fit only for spitting out.'[11]

So hot water and cold water were beneficial, lukewarm water was useless. The analogy is obvious. The Laodicean church was bringing no benefit to the community or culture. They were not being a faithful witness. Their riches and wealth were of no spiritual benefit. They are exhorted to let Jesus in, hear his voice and become overcomers.

These letters to the seven churches are exhortations to the church in every age. He who has an ear let him hear what the Spirit says to the churches. The message for us today is to make sure we adhere to the following:
1. Don't compromise with the world, the flesh and the devil.
2. Don't be complacent about earthly riches.

3. Recognize and deal with the Jezebelic spirit.
4. Don't be super-spiritual.
5. Don't be lukewarm.

God disciplines and brings judgment to his church to refine and purify. The fires of tribulation, persecution and opposition help to strengthen the church. There are times when he will bring his judgments. Such words as 'I will throw her on a bed of sickness . . . I will kill her children with pestilence' (Revelation 2:22, 23 NASB) should make us realize that if we are unrepentant, God will act.

This is a realistic picture of how the church has been throughout its history, but the visions of Revelation give us a hope that she will be purified, perfected and made ready for the coming of Jesus.

Let us build the church according to biblical principle, in the power of the Holy Spirit, and see a glorious end-time church challenging the darkness of the world living without God.

BUILD YOUR CHURCH AND HEAL THIS LAND

We are your people, who are called by your name
We call upon you now, to declare your fame.
In this nation of darkness, you have called us to be light
As we seek your face now, stir up your might.

Build your church and heal this land
Let your kingdom come
Build your church and heal this land
Let your will be done.
(Copyright © 1986 Thankyou Music)[12]

CHAPTER 5
WELCOME TO THE THRONE ROOM
Read Revelation 4 and 5

We now come to a new vision in Revelation 4:1: 'After this I looked, and behold, a door standing open in heaven' (ESV).

In these two chapters we get a glimpse into the throne room. I have placed these two chapters under four headings to help us understand it.

AT THE THRONE OF THE KINGDOM THERE ARE PERSPECTIVES AND MYSTERIES OF ETERNAL GOVERNMENT

We are introduced to more numerical symbolism, which helps us understand the connection between the Old Testament and the New Testament church.

The number 24. In chapter 4 and verse 4 we see 24 thrones and 24 elders. This could be a reference to the 12 sons of Israel and the 12 apostles. It could also be a reference to a key time in Israel's history.

In 1 Chronicles 15 David, who has now replaced Saul as king, has defeated the Jebusites and is now occupying Jerusalem.

The Ark of the Covenant, the symbol of God's presence is now restored to its rightful place in the midst of God's people.

Just as Moses, in a previous generation, had been given instructions by God about how the tabernacle should be built and how the priesthood was to function, so now in the time of David, the tabernacle and the Ark of the Covenant were to become the focal point in worship for the whole nation of Israel, the prototype of God's people. This anticipated the time when worship would rise from every tribe, tongue and nation as described in Revelation.

The first Book of Chronicles gives us a vivid picture of what this looked like. David appointed chief musicians and their families, who were divided into 24 teams. They were trained in singing, playing instruments and prophesying. Each of these 24 teams would have had 12 members of their family (making 288 in total), leading the singing of the psalms and expressing their worship. In 1 Chronicles 15 we receive a full account of the dynamic, prophetic creativity of worship at David's tabernacle. The connection with John's vision in Revelation is that he saw 24 elders with harps singing the song of the Lamb and leading the heavenly praise.

The 24 elders, reminiscent of the 24 teams of musical priests, seems to speak of the completeness of the church at worship.

This theme occurs again in Revelation 19.

The next number is seven. The number seven has always held a fascination. Mathematicians call it a prime number which means that it can only be divided by itself and by the number one. It had significance in the Ancient World as a number speaking of completion. The Bible speaks of the seven days of creation (six days plus a rest day to complete the seven and so we get seven days in a week). We speak of the seven pillars of wisdom, the Seven Wonders of the world, sailing the Seven Seas. Apparently, the human mind is able to receive and retain seven pieces of information. (Of course, for many it could be more, but this is a basic premise.)

It is easier to retain seven digits in the memory than any other number. Biblically it is significant, speaking of wholeness and completion.

In Revelation 4 we have the seven lamps of fire. We have already referred to the lampstand in connection with the seven churches, but here we have a lampstand in heaven burning with the seven spirits of God, the Holy Spirit.

Isaiah 11:1-2 (NKJV) says:

'There shall come forth a Rod from the stem of Jesse, and a Branch will grow out of his roots. The Spirit of the LORD will rest on Him, the Spirit of wisdom and understanding, the Spirit of counsel and might, the Spirit of knowledge and of the fear of the LORD.'

The perfection and power of God's presence by his Spirit is represented by these seven characteristics.

The next significant number is four. The four living creatures around the throne each have four eyes front and back. The number four again speaks of the whole earth, four rivers from the garden of Eden. The four points of the compass, the four winds in Ezekiel's valley of the dry bones.

The four living creatures, the Lion – strength, the Ox – service and humility, Man – intelligence, the Eagle – swiftness, speak of and represent the rule of God over the whole of creation.

The other things we see around the throne are the emerald rainbow and sea of glass like crystal. The rainbow reminds us of the covenant of mercy made with Noah after the flood.

The crystal sea of glass is a reference to a huge metal circular basin which could hold 8,000 gallons of water, which was in the courtyard of Solomon's Temple. It was believed to represent the Red Sea which was both a symbol of deliverance for Israel and judgment on the Egyptians. The sea often speaks of the reality of evil in biblical imagery. Later in Revelation the beast comes out of the sea. For John the sea was a place of separation. The presence of this crystal sea in the throne room gives us a picture of the 'stilling of the seas' from a heavenly perspective. It speaks of God's victory over evil and his righteous judgments.

The symbolism of all this reminds us of the Old Testament events and God's sovereign ruling over them. This vision is also redolent of Ezekiel's vision. The consistency of visual imagery throughout the Bible brings an incredible sense of cohesion in the way God communicates with us. He speaks through stories, characters, events and visual imagery. A big question for us is: when in history do the events of this vision take place? At what point in time do we get this glimpse into heaven? The futurists believe this is the beginning of the last days leading up to Christ's return.

However, Revelation is neither exclusively a history book nor a futuristic book. It deals with past, present and future. It is an unfolding of God's purpose and has an ongoing application for us.

In view of this we need to understand something about heaven to get the full impact of the vision. The Bible uses the concept of heaven in different ways:

1. It is a place where the birds fly, where we look up and see the sky.
2. It is a place where the stars and the planets are, where we see the sun and moon.
3. It is a place where the saints go when they die. 'Today you will be with me in paradise', words spoken by Jesus to the dying thief (Luke 23:43 NIV).
4. It will be our eternal home when Jesus returns. We will be in the new heavens and the new earth.
5. 'The heavenly places' – a place of supernatural activity that exists in the present. It is a place where the activity of God, the angels, the devil and demons exist. Job 2:1 (KJV) says: 'There was a day when the sons of God came to present themselves before the LORD, and Satan also came among them.' (This explains the mystery of Satan. Later in Revelation we see when he was cast out of heaven.)

All this speaks of the supernatural realm. God exists in this dimension and we do too. It is a great mystery, which is why Revelation includes visions and pictures. We get an impression.

Revelation is a book that unfolds the history of redemption, so in this supernatural world we have a vision of a throne, precious stones, a rainbow, four living creatures with eyes everywhere, cherubim, seraphim, myriads of angels, a crystal sea and as the vision unfolds much, much more.

AT THE THRONE OF THE KINGDOM THERE IS A GOD WHO UNVEILS THE PANORAMA OF HISTORY

History teaches us that history teaches man nothing. There are many examples of this, such as when Hitler made exactly the same mistake as Napoleon when he attacked Russia. Neither allowed for the harshness of the Russian winter and so both were defeated.

In the 1930s there was a famous newsreel which proclaimed that the destiny of the world was in the hands of Hitler, Mussolini and Stalin. As the events of that time unfolded before the world, it became obvious that these rulers were evil despots. Today we have politicians and leaders who make all sorts of claims about their political ideas, from the extreme left to the extreme right.

There are many who are crying out for leadership at this time. It is true we must pray for leadership on a world scale, but the answer to the world's problems is not found in political ideology or secular world leaders. We will look at that more carefully in the later chapters of Revelation.

Daniel 2:20-21 (NASB) says:

'Let the name of God be blessed forever and ever, for wisdom and power belong to Him. It is He who changes times and epochs; He removes kings and establishes kings; He gives wisdom to wise men and knowledge to men of understanding.'

History is directed and ordered by God who knows the end from the beginning. History is heading for a divinely directed goal. Ephesians 1:9-10 says He is 'making known to us the mystery of his will, according to his purpose, which he set forth in Christ as a plan for the fullness of time, to unite ['*anakephalaioomai*'] all things in him, things in heaven and things on earth' (ESV). The Greek word for unite is better translated as a 'summing up'. Rather like an accountant looking at income and expenditure and drawing conclusions from the evidence before him. Kittel says of this word: 'To bring to a conclusion, a definitive, comprehensive and recapitulatory summation of the totality of things as the church receives its head. In Christ, this head, the totality is comprehended afresh as its sum.'[13]

The Lordship of Christ over the whole of history is one of the great themes of the Book of Revelation and this verse in Ephesians 1:10 is yet another way of expressing this great truth.

The events of history and the judgments of God that will appear as history unfolds are contained in a scroll or a book with seven seals.

In Revelation 5:2, the angel asks the question: 'Who is worthy to open the book?' (NASB). In other words, who can explain history? (We will see when the book is opened that the events of history unfold before us.) At first, there is no one who can open the book. This is rather like the dilemma the world has faced with coronavirus. Who has an answer? John wept – there are many weeping now.

AT THE THRONE OF THE KINGDOM THERE IS A KING WHO REVEALS THE PARADOX OF VICTORY

In Revelation 5:5 the angel says: 'Do not weep. Behold, the Lion of the tribe of Judah, the Root of David has prevailed to open the scroll and loose its seven seals' (NKJV).

Why is Jesus called the Lion of Judah?

In Genesis 49:8-10 when Jacob blesses his sons he says:

'Judah, you are he whom your brothers shall praise; your hand shall be on the neck of your enemies; your father's children shall bow down before you. Judah is a lion's whelp; from the prey, my son, you have gone up. He bows down, he lies down as a lion; and as a lion, who shall rouse him? The sceptre shall not depart from Judah, nor a lawgiver from between his feet until Shiloh comes.' (NKJV)

This blessing of Jacob over his son Judah is a key prophecy concerning the eventual coming of the Messiah. The prophecy would be fulfilled firstly in the coming of David and the establishing of the kingdom under his rulership. It speaks of the promise that God has for the whole world and not just for the nation of Israel. The promise given to Abraham many years before this, that 'all the families of the earth will be blessed' (Genesis 12:3 NASB), pointed to a greater purpose than just the nation of Israel. The making of Israel into a great nation was a step towards a much greater fulfilment of God's plan in the whole earth. The prophecy goes beyond the establishing of the Davidic kingdom. One day a ruler would come from the royal line of David who would completely fulfil Jacob's prophecy. Although David would partially fulfil this prophecy, many of the psalms point beyond the nation of Israel to a much greater spiritual nation that would encompass the whole earth and 'great David's greater son' would come and fulfil this Messianic kingly rule to establish a government that would reach the ends of the earth. David and Israel were the prototype of what God would eventually do. There are so many prophetic psalms that proclaim this theme. For instance, Psalm 68, a great Messianic psalm, ends with the declaration, 'Sing to God, O kingdoms of the earth' (NASB).

This theme is repeated over and over again in the psalms and the prophets. So, at the throne of the kingdom where John sees Jesus as the Lion of Judah, he sees him as the mighty, victorious king who was prophesied by Abraham, Jacob, David, Isaiah and the rest of the prophets. The Lion of Judah roars his victory over every nation of the earth as he exercises his governmental authority from the throne. In yet another Messianic prophecy, Psalm 2:7-9 declares:

'I will declare the decree: the LORD has said to Me, "You are My Son, today I have begotten You. Ask of Me, and I will give You the nations for Your inheritance, and the ends of the earth for Your possession. You shall break them with a rod of iron; You shall dash them to pieces like a potter's vessel.' (NKJV)

Jesus the Lion of Judah is worthy to take the book.

History is moving towards the glorious conclusion where the Lion will roar over the whole of creation and Jesus returns. Now, here is the paradox.

Revelation 5:6-7 (NKJV) says:

'And I looked, and behold, in the midst of the throne and of the four living creatures, and in the midst of the elders, stood a Lamb as though it had been slain having seven horns and seven eyes, which are the seven spirits of God sent out into all the earth. Then He came and took the scroll out of the right hand of Him who sat on the throne.'

The Lamb who forever bears the marks of the sacrifice on Calvary will be an eternal reminder that we are saved through the death of the Lamb. The way to this rulership and victory would be through the Lamb of God, taking away the sins of the world. Victory comes through the suffering of the cross. We will only have an entrance into this throne room by the blood of the Lamb. Jesus, throughout eternity, will bear the marks of his suffering as an eternal reminder of the price paid for our salvation. As lines from the great hymn 'Crown Him with Many Crowns' express it: 'Those wounds yet visible above, in beauty glorified.'[14]

Notice here also the connection between the Lamb and the Spirit. In the Old Testament, after the sacrifice was prepared and placed on the altar, fire would fall and consume the sacrifice.

Through Calvary, the resurrection and the ascension, the Spirit has been poured out on us in response to what Jesus the Lamb has accomplished in our salvation. As Charles Wesley put it: 'The Spirit answers to the blood and tells me I've been born of God.'[15]

We see the Lamb with the seven eyes (symbolically all-seeing), looking over the whole earth. We are reminded that the earth is the Lord's. Jesus has all authority. It does not belong to Satan and never has.

When we look at the state of the world, we can get depressed, and events such as the coronavirus pandemic can provoke a sombre mood. For us as believers we have the glorious hope that the Lion of Judah is roaring his victory, that the Lamb has the book in his hand and is in total control. It is no surprise that all heaven bursts into praise, but it is not just heaven.

AT THE THRONE OF THE KINGDOM THERE IS A PEOPLE FOR ETERNITY

In the song of praise in Revelation 5:9-10 we are invited to join in the song of the heavenly creatures, the angels, the 24 elders and the myriads of angelic beings.

The prayers of the saints fill the golden bowls of incense. We are participants through prayer and praise in this heavenly activity now, here on earth.

God is forming a people from every tribe, tongue and nation, a kingdom of priests, reigning in life. A people cleansed by the blood, redeemed by the blood, delivered by the blood, overcoming by the blood, fellowshipping with one another as the blood of Jesus cleanses us from all sin. In 1 Peter 2:9-10 these people are described:

'But you are a chosen generation, a royal priesthood, a holy nation, His own special people, that you may proclaim the praises of Him who called you out of darkness into His marvellous light; who once were not a people but are now the people of God, who had not obtained mercy but now have obtained mercy.' (NKJV)

This wonderful description of the people of God has all been made possible because of the vision and events described by John in Revelation 4 and 5. Revelation 5:12-13 declares:

'Worthy is the Lamb who was slain to receive power and riches and wisdom, and strength and honour and glory and blessing . . . blessing and honour and glory and power be to Him who sits on the throne, and to the Lamb, forever and ever!' (NKJV)

CHAPTER 6
UNDERSTANDING THE ONGOING
JUDGMENTS OF GOD

Read Revelation 6:1-17 and Romans 8:18-25

When coronavirus broke out many were asking if the Bible had anything to say. The sceptics may well ask, how does a God of love allow such suffering? This is a question that the human race has always wrestled with.

In answering this we need a biblical overview about how God views the world in which we live and our place in it. Whenever there is some kind of disaster, whether it is war, earthquakes, outbreaks of terrorism, the refugee crisis, natural disasters or human suffering of any kind, it is important for us to see what the Bible teaches.

There will be some who have a simplistic understanding of faith that believes God always heals and protects and who will quote their proof texts to justify their position. There are others who believe that such calamitous events as the fires in Australia, the flooding in the UK, or historically the outbreak of HIV and other major health issues are demonstrations of God's wrath and judgment. There will be yet others who see this current situation as a fulfilment of biblical prophecy and that the coming of Jesus is going to happen very soon.

There may well be grains of truth in some of these points of view, but if we are going to understand what the Bible really teaches it is important not to take isolated passages and so-called 'proof texts', but to try and understand the big picture that we get in God's word.

The Old Testament points to the coming of Jesus and his mission to bring salvation to a world that is under the curse of sin. As well as personal sins that we have all committed, the human race has to endure such things as terrorism, war, greed and other terrible inhumane practices. We see from this that the human race and creation itself is out of joint with the Creator.

The result of the fall in Genesis meant that not only was the human race separated from God because of Adam's sin and rebellion, but the consequence of his sinfulness means that the whole of creation is affected. The effect of the fall on creation covers everything including earthquakes, tsunamis, famine, viruses and plagues.

The big story of the Bible is that Jesus came not only to redeem us from our sins, but also to redeem the whole of creation. A day is coming when Jesus will return and those who have been redeemed will be forever with him in the new, restored heavens and earth. Those who are saved now will be there.

A passage of Scripture for understanding the disjointedness of creation is Romans 8:18-23. Here Paul states that the whole of creation waits with eager longing for the revealing of the sons of God. He goes on to say that the creation at the moment is subject to futility and is in bondage to corruption.

The whole of creation is under the judgment of God because of the sinfulness of man. This judgment is general, not specific. We should understand that God is not being specific in his judgment by sending such disasters as famine or coronavirus. If somebody dies because of the virus it does not mean that God is bringing a harsh judgment on them. Good people and bad people will be affected because of the general judgment of God over the whole world. God's common grace and his restraining love for the whole of humanity stand in juxtaposition to his general judgments. Mankind is sinful, creation is affected. God loves the world and his common grace benefits the whole of mankind, but his judgments are also seen. That is why Jesus came as a redeemer to save and deliver from this present evil world and give us an eternal hope of the new heaven and new earth.

Meanwhile the world has to face pandemics like coronavirus as well as all kinds of natural disasters.

When the disciples asked Jesus about the signs of his coming in Matthew 24, in what is commonly known as the 'Olivet discourse', his reply in verses 6 to 8 reveals an outline of future events and of divine judgments upon the world. His answer pointed towards the fall of Jerusalem in AD 70 but he also indicated the signs which will precede his coming.

Matthew 24:6-8 (ESV):

'And you will hear of wars and rumours of wars. See that you are not alarmed, for this must take place, but the end is not yet. For nation will rise against nation, and kingdom against kingdom, and there will be famines and earthquakes in various places. All these are but the beginning of the birth pains.' (Greek 'arche odinon')

Anthony A. Hoekema in his book *The Bible and the Future* says:

'These are not strictly speaking signs of the end, for Jesus says plainly about these signs that when they take place people must not be alarmed for "the end is not yet." He says all these are the beginning of birth pains. The expression here used became a technical term in rabbinic literature to describe the period of suffering preceding messianic deliverance.'[16]

Kittel comments on the usage of this word in Matthew 24 and also in Mark 13.

'Afflictions will usher in the end times, although when they occur one must not over-hastily expect the end. Matthew 24:8

relates "beginnings of sorrows" to all the eschatological woes that precede the new birth of the world; they indicate the imminence of the time of salvation."[17]

There is a similar statement in Luke 21 which includes pestilences in the list. This could be translated plagues or even viruses. These events are to be considered as 'signs of the times', in other words things that will happen on the earth before he comes again (including coronavirus).

There are references to these times in many of the Old Testament prophecies and they seem to point to the time between Christ's first and second coming. Jesus says these signs must not alarm us because the end is not yet.

The 'last days' is the period between Christ's ascension and the Second Coming. (There are many eminent theologians and Bible scholars who would take this view.) So, it would seem that in Jesus's Olivet discourse he is describing the things we can expect to be happening in the period of time between his first and his second coming. He is unfolding history in advance of it happening.

These signs are evidence that God, in his sovereign rule, is continually bringing judgments on earth. This does not mean that people who undergo suffering or death as a result of disasters like wars, famines, earthquakes, tsunamis, pestilences (like coronavirus) are being singled out as objects of God's wrath.

In Luke 13:4, Jesus shows us that when the tower of the pool of Siloam fell and killed eighteen people, they were no better or worse than anyone else. He then gives a challenge to all to repent. The judgment was general not specific, but the call to repentance was for all.

It would seem in Jesus's eschatological discourse that he is showing that God's judgments are continually being poured out on a fallen world, until he returns.

The call to a fallen humanity to return to God is as strong as ever for 'God so loved the world, that he gave his only Son, that whoever believes in him should not perish' (John 3:16 ESV).

Our understanding should be that these signs point towards the fact that Jesus is returning. This means for us that when we experience these painful situations, including coronavirus, that God is actually working out his purpose in history.

Fear should have no place in us. These things are the birth pangs heralding a better world.

Romans 8:22 says: 'We know that the whole creation has been groaning as in the pains of childbirth right up to the present moment' (NIV). The second verb here, '*synodinei*', is from the same root as the word '*odinon*' (meaning 'birth pains', quoted earlier in Matthew 24:8).

It would seem that coronavirus is one of the signs of the groaning of creation. It is therefore vital for us to see what else Romans 8 says to us in response to this to encourage us in these difficult days.

Having given us an understanding of the groaning of creation and likening that to the pains of childbirth, Paul encourages us to pray. He says: 'Not only this, but also we ourselves . . . groan within ourselves' (Romans 8:23 NASB).

There is a depth of prayer and intercession that goes beyond words.

The teaching in Romans is permeated with the Holy Spirit, bringing freedom from condemnation and giving us a quality of life in our salvation that brings deliverance from the law of sin and death.

Another aspect of the Spirit's work within us is that he enables us to pray. It is in moments of deep agony of soul that the Holy Spirit takes over and intercedes through us.

The creation is groaning, awaiting the judgments on a creation out of joint with its creator. This is in anticipation of that glorious day when all things will change forever. 'For I consider that the sufferings of this present time are not worthy to be compared with the glory that is to be revealed to us' (Romans 8:18 NASB).

This is 'big picture theology' which should motivate us to pray with passion and fervency. God has a cosmic plan into which our lives fit. Creation groans awaiting a glorious outcome. Although prayer is a joyful experience, there are times when it can be intense, with tears and with our being touched with the pain of the Father's heart for a lost world.

My grandfather, who was a great man of prayer, used to say to me when I was a little boy, when you pray it must be more than your 'going to bed prayers'. Now I am the same age as he was when he told me this, I have a greater understanding of what he meant. We have been given the Holy Spirit to help us in our weakness, so that we can pray 'in the Spirit'.

The gift of tongues can be a helpful way in which we do this. Paul said that when we pray in a tongue, we speak mysteries to God (1 Corinthians 14:2).

If we are concerned about the state of the world, the violence, the turmoil, the uncertainty, we need to learn to pray in the Spirit. We need the same passion to pray for people to be saved, and for the church to be more outreaching to the lost.

During my life and ministry, many times I have been in situations where I have not known what to do. I have been driven to earnest fervent prayer. At times I have not been able to articulate my words, but a combination of deep groanings and tongues of intercession have brought me through to a place of faith to see answers.

One of the many examples I could relate concerned a church I was helping which had a leadership crisis. There seemed to be no way forward, and one night I was awakened at three in the morning with a song I used to sing as a child in the Salvation Army.

Keep the touch of God on your soul
Keep the touch of God on your soul.
Go wrestle fight and pray
Until the break of day
And keep the touch of God on your soul.[18]

I felt the Holy Spirit say: 'Get up, get dressed and pray until daybreak.' I obeyed what I felt God was telling me to do and went out into the dark early morning hours to pray. I battled for the situation with groanings, tongues, cries and times of silence.

When eventually dawn broke I felt God say to me, 'You can stop now.' At that very moment a gust of wind blew across my face and a storm broke in our area. Again I heard God speak and say about the situation I was praying for, 'There will be a big storm but you will ride it out.'

Over the next few months, what God had spoken came to pass.

In these days of uncertainty, we need more than our 'going to bed prayers'. The creation is out of joint, it is groaning. We need the groans of the Spirit as we give ourselves to intercession. We will see later in the Book of Revelation that the intercessions of the church are like incense that moves the heart of God to act.

Another significant theme we can draw from Romans 8 in regard to his judgments is his sovereign will over the world and over our lives. It is both cosmic and personal.

Dr David Campbell says:

'God in his sovereignty uses even the evil purposes of the enemy in a fallen world and turns them for his good. His purpose in using such calamities is twofold: to awaken a complacent and compromised church, and mercifully to warn a rebellious world by such judgments that a worse judgment is coming and so to repent and escape it.'[19]

Whatever happens we can be certain that God always has a plan that he is working out. Let us be sure of our faith in these difficult days. Romans 8:38-39 (NLT) says:

'And I am convinced that nothing can ever separate us from God's love. Neither death nor life, neither angels nor demons, neither our fears for today nor our worries about tomorrow – not even the powers of hell can separate us from God's love. No power in the sky above or in the earth below – indeed, nothing in all creation will ever be able to separate us from the love of God that is revealed in Christ Jesus our Lord.'

CHAPTER 7
THE SEALS BREAK
Read Revelation 6:1 – 8:6

We are invited by one of the four living creatures from the throne, who speaks with a voice like thunder, to come and see the Lamb, who has been declared worthy to open the seals of the book. We have already seen that the book is an unfolding of the panorama of world history, and as the seals are broken one by one, we get the detail of what this looks like.

Revelation chapter 6 to chapter 8:6 describes the breaking of the seven seals, then from chapter 8:6 to chapter 11 the sounding of the seven trumpets is announced.

These two sections are not chronological but parallel and are events which take place throughout world history. We will find that the seals and the trumpets are saying similar things and they parallel the teaching that we see in Mark 13 where Jesus takes Peter, James, John and Andrew aside to explain what was going to happen in the world after his death and resurrection (although they were not able to fully understand what was going to happen to him).

The teaching Jesus gave outlined the type of things that would be happening in the world before he returned 'coming in clouds with great power and glory'. The vision that John receives all these years later would have jogged his memory of that day on the Mount of Olives.

THE JUDGMENTS

The first seal

John has a vision of a white horse. Sitting on it was a conqueror with a bow. He also had a crown on his head. It has been suggested, due to the fact that the horse is white, that this conqueror is actually Jesus since he does appear later in the book riding on a white horse. However, this is not logical. The fact that the horse is white could indicate that this is a false Christ, something that Jesus himself said would happen.

These four horsemen are riding together, which links with Zechariah 6 where the prophet has several apocalyptic visions. Also, Jesus the Lamb breaks the seal that unleashes the horsemen. The natural and political disasters are caused by Christ in order to judge unbelievers who persecute Christians, in order to vindicate his people. It is Jesus who authorizes these horsemen to ride out.

The rider of this white horse goes out to seek power through warfare. The crown on his head speaks of a ruling over others. It speaks of imperialism and empire-building through violence. There have been many in history who have gone forth to conquer other nations through warfare, thinking that they will be creating a new, idealistic way of life for the people they are conquering. Jesus said there would be wars and rumours of wars and here the rider of the white horse sets out to gain dominion over others through warfare.

The second seal
This horse is red, and the rider is given authority and power to take peace from the earth through people slaying each other. This seems to speak of civil wars which can be particularly brutal. In England in the seventeenth century the Civil War between Parliament and the monarchy saw intransigence on both sides.

The King, Charles I, was influenced by his Catholic wife and was steering the Church of England back towards Catholicism.

Along with Archbishop Laud he sought to bring changes to how the church should worship and introduced a new prayer book. This was unacceptable to the evangelical, reformed Puritans, and particularly caused outrage in Scotland where the Covenanters rejected the new prayer book. Charles tried to raise an army to invade Scotland, but failed. The seeds were sown for a violent civil war.

Although Puritanism was a strong spiritual movement, producing many excellent theological thinkers and reformers, the outworking of some aspects of their belief went beyond what Scripture teaches. Spiritually there was a mixture of godliness and intolerance, as demonstrated by Cromwell's actions in Ireland. This period in English history demonstrated that Christian living cannot be controlled by political ideology. Puritanism was a strange mixture of sound theology, accompanied by a cruel outworking at times. The English Civil War is a blight on its history with neither side covering itself in glory.

The same problem can be seen in the world today where Christians align themselves with a political party to impose Christian morality. The danger of civil unrest lurks uneasily.

In the nineteenth century, the American Civil War, fought over the issue of slavery, was brutal. Its effects on America can be felt even today, with issues of racism still lying under the surface.

In 1947 the war between India and Pakistan left a political situation that still festers today, and in recent history the war in the Balkans was particularly brutal. The rider of the red horse will continue to ride out, removing peace from nations and undermining the brotherhood of national identity.

The third seal
The third seal sees a black horse released with the rider holding a pair of scales. A voice from the midst of the four living creatures calls out: 'A quart of wheat for a denarius, and three quarts of barley for a denarius' (Revelation 6:6 NASB). A denarius would be about a day's wages.

This speaks of economic collapse, a scarcity of food and basic necessities. Inflation and the divide between the rich and the poor are suggested by this. The oil and the wine are symbols of the good life and yet they are not touched.

In the UK, during the coronavirus pandemic, the government made provision for people who could not work due to the restrictions on the companies and organisations they were working for. The furloughing scheme was a lifesaver for many who would have had no income.

If the reports are to be believed, there were extremely rich, big business tycoons furloughing their staff while they spent time on their luxury yachts.

Other Western countries have had different schemes, and yet others had no schemes at all, meaning that the economic collapse has caused all kinds of hardship.

The fourth seal
The fourth seal sees the release of a pale horse who was called Death and Hades. This rider was given authority over a quarter of the earth to kill with the sword, with hunger and with death. These represent various social upheavals and problems. There is a terrible rise in knife crime, there is poverty and there are situations where food is scarce. In a BBC report, the World Food Programme (WFP) has shown that the world faces a possible 'food pandemic'. The statistics reveal that severe food shortages will affect 73 million in African nations, 43 million in the Middle East and Asia, and 18.5 million in Latin America and the Caribbean. We tend to think of famine and food shortage as Third World issues, but even in affluent Europe the problem could affect up to half a million people. Recently in the UK the coronavirus pandemic has highlighted food shortages in many areas where without the provision of foodbanks, many families living

in poverty would go hungry. These problems are not just Third World issues. The word for death here (Revelation 6:8) is 'thanatos' which is the word used to translate the Hebrew word for plague in the Greek Old Testament. Some translations actually translate the word 'death' as pestilence or disease. Throughout the centuries there have been terrible plagues which have decimated the population of nations. At the moment it seems that the pale horse is galloping at speed through the nations of the earth.

Another aspect of the death brought by the pale horse could be those who have taken up their cross in a particular way and suffered and died for their faith.

The fifth seal
The breaking of the fifth seal has a very different feel from the judgments of the first four. This reveals the souls of martyrs who throughout history have suffered and died for their faith. It would seem there is a special place for them in eternity. Their cry, 'How long?' is not a cry for revenge but for the justice of a righteous God. Their place under the altar, in Jewish tradition, was a place of the highest honour and speaks of the presence of God. Their reward will be great, and they are now in the presence of the Lord awaiting the coming day of judgment.

The sixth seal
The sixth seal being opened seems to be a summing up of the cataclysmic events on earth leading up to Jesus's return. We are at the climax of history. Everything is being shaken, the Parousia or Second Coming is about to happen. This links again with Jesus's teaching in Mark 13.

Hebrews 12:25-29 also makes a reference to these events. The description of what will happen is an exhortation to us as believers not to waver, but to be ready. It says:

'See that you do not refuse Him who speaks. For if they did not escape who refused Him who spoke on earth, much more shall we not escape if we turn away from Him who speaks from heaven, whose voice then shook the earth; but now He has promised, saying, "Yet once more I shake not only the earth, but also heaven." Now this, "Yet once more," indicates the removal of those things that are being shaken, as of things that are made, that the things which cannot be shaken may remain. Therefore, since we are receiving a kingdom which cannot be shaken, let us have grace, by which we may serve God acceptably with reverence and godly fear. For our God is a consuming fire.' (NKJV)

The opening of this seal is the first of seven descriptions of judgment in Revelation and the end.

As the sky recedes like a scroll, and every mountain and island is moved out of place, no one can escape. Kings of the earth, great men, commanders, mighty men, slaves, free men, everyone from all classes of humanity will experience this great day of the wrath of the Lamb.

THE INTERLUDE, RESTRAINT AND PROTECTION

Before the seventh seal is broken, we have an interlude which shows the church is safe amid all the drama of these cataclysmic events, and God has a glorious plan for it.

The vision begins with four angels at the four corners of the earth holding back the four winds.

RESTRAINT

The apocalyptic horsemen are loosed but the four angels restrain them. Even when God sends his judgments, evil can only go as far as he allows.

There is an important pastoral principle for us here. We sometimes go through an evil day, but God is in control. We have the weapons of prayer and the Word, the gifts of the Spirit and supernatural breakthroughs of the Spirit, but often we need to fight in prayer for these things. In Ephesians 6:13 we are called to 'withstand in the evil day' (NKJV).

We need to remember that the timing of the lifting of the coronavirus or any other disaster is in the hands of God. We can pray and he will act in his timing.

PROTECTION

Another angel appears and tells the four angels not to harm the earth and the sea until God's people have been sealed.

There are two groupings of people here, the 144,000 representing the 12 tribes of Israel.

The 144,00 = 12 tribes x 12 apostles, which is the community of faith through the ages and a great multitude which no one could number, of all nations, tribes, peoples and tongues.

We need to take both groupings as two aspects of the same thing. All of these together represent the true church of God in all ages. The first representation is symbolic in nature, and the second picture represents the actual multitude of the saints. The symbolism of 144,000 (the 12 tribes), and the multitude, is inclusive of all the people of God who are sealed. The church is the continuation of the true Israel. This helps us to make sense of the Old Testament and particularly the prophets.

In Ephesians 2:14-16 Paul says:

'For He Himself is our peace, who has made both one, and has broken down the middle wall of separation, having abolished in His flesh the enmity, that is, the law of commandments contained in ordinances, so as to create in Himself one new man from the two, thus making peace, and that He might reconcile them both to God in one body through the cross, thereby putting to death the enmity.' (NKJV)

It is clear that the division between Jew and Gentile has been abolished through the cross. Israel is no longer to be regarded as the people of God. The gospel regards saved Jews and saved Gentiles as 'one new man'. The Book of Revelation brings Jews and Gentiles together as the people of God, the church.

In his commentary on this verse G.K. Beale says: 'The prophecies about Israel's restoration to its land began to be fulfilled in unbelieving Jews and Gentiles being restored to God through Christ, and thus coming to represent the true Israel and the New Jerusalem.'[20]

The protection is from God himself. The protective sealing is prefigured in the Exodus story of the Passover when the blood of the Lamb was placed on the door lintels so the angel of death would pass over that house. The blood of Christ is for God to see. We have protection because God sees the blood of Jesus rather than our sin.

The sealing of protection is also prefigured in Ezekiel 9 where the city was about to be invaded as a judgment of God upon a rebellious and idolatrous people. However, those who had remained faithful and righteous were given a mark, a seal, that gave them protection against this imminent disaster. The protection is spiritual.

Believers and unbelievers suffer similar trials, physical afflictions and life's difficulties because we live in a fallen world. However, these trials can either purify us or harden our hearts. If we are Christians, we have spiritual protection in every circumstance. (Of course, we can pray for deliverance and healing. It is important to balance the fact that God is sovereign and will teach us through every circumstance, but he also demonstrates his love and power through healing and deliverance. It is important to hold these truths in tension.)

The sealing occurs again in chapter 14 and we will also see that there is a countersealing, the mark of the beast. We will look at that in a later chapter.

2 Timothy 2:19 gives us an indication as to what God's seal is: 'The firm foundation of God stands, having this seal, "The Lord knows those who are His," and, "Everyone who names the name of the Lord is to abstain from wickedness."' (NASB).

We have his name written over us, so we are sealed, protected by the name of the Lord. It is a seal of authentication. A royal document receives a royal seal which authenticates that it is from the monarch. It is a seal of identity. In Ephesians 1, Paul says that we are sealed with the Holy Spirit who is the guarantee of our inheritance. The word 'guarantee' is a down-payment of our future in the present. He brings the reality of the future into the present.

The seal empowers us, protects us, authenticates us. This goes on all through the trials, pressures and tribulations of life.

As John Newton says in his great hymn 'Amazing Grace':

Through many dangers toils and snares
We have already come.
'Twas grace that brought us safe thus far
And grace will lead me home.[21]

There are four vital questions regarding the 'sealing' arising out of the implications of the passage.

1. Do we have assurance of salvation?
2. Do we desire to live in obedience?
3. When we fail, do we live a life of ongoing repentance?
4. Are we actively witnessing for Christ even amidst the pressures of opposition?

In conclusion to the interlude in Revelation 7 we gain a wonderful vision of the church combining verses 1-8 and 9-16. The church is:

1. Rescued (from the ongoing tribulation)
2. Cleansed (robes washed white in the blood of the Lamb)
3. Worshipping (serving day and night in the temple)
4. Enjoying God's presence
5. Receiving God's provision
6. Receiving God's guidance
7. Joyful (every tear wiped from their eyes)

This is for us now but will be ours in eternity also. This is the church in victory at his coming. Let's aim to be this kind of church.

THE FINALE

The seventh seal: 'There was silence in heaven for half an hour'
It is as though the play is over and the curtain is open for the final appearance of the cast and the final bow. However, the stage remains empty.

Sometimes when we pray, we can feel the silence of heaven. How do we handle that?

Surely by faith that God will speak through the Scriptures, or by a word of encouragement, or through our circumstances, or even the whisper into our own soul. However, there are times when he keeps us waiting.

At this stage, as the vision progresses, we are not shown the details of the events at which we have arrived.

We are left with the pause button pressed, in a state of anticipation. We will have to wait for more detail of the vision to be disclosed.

CHAPTER 8
THE TRUMPETS SOUND
Read Revelation 8:6 – 11:15

THE DRAMA RERUN

After the silence in heaven we see seven angels with trumpets and an angel with a golden censer holding the incense of the prayers of the saints. It reminds us that our prayers affect what is happening. As we pray, God acts.

The seven trumpets are reminiscent of the seven priests with trumpets marching round the walls of Jericho. Was the fact they had to march round in silence prophetic symbolism for the silence in heaven before the trumpets sounded?

The seven trumpets of Revelation develop what the seals have shown us, but with greater intensity. The seals have already brought us the warnings but when the trumpets sound, they are like a stentorian call adding judgment to what has gone before.

These judgments are proclaimed, bringing:

1. Disasters on the earth.
2. Disasters on the seas.
3. Disasters in the rivers.
4. Disasters in the heavens.
5. Psychological, emotional and mental disasters. (One of the biggest issues today is mental health. Has it always been as big as it is today or is it just that we are more aware of it? Or, do the stresses of modern life create the mental health issues? Whatever the answer, it is clear Revelation prophesies this would happen.)
6. Disasters affecting the whole of mankind.

After the first trumpets sound, with the fourth trumpet comes an angelic cry of 'Woe, woe, woe' and the next three trumpet calls tell us what those woes are. The fifth and sixth trumpets repeat the message of the seals but using different language as they expand the vision. What is implied by these trumpets are ecological disasters, pollution and such things as oil spills, Chernobyl and other issues to do with the degrading of Planet Earth. G.K. Beale's and David Campbell's comment on the sounding of this trumpet is graphic.

'The trumpet blast sets in motion an horrific army of locusts energized by demonic sources. The imagery derives from Exodus 10 and Joel 2:1-11, where a literal locust plague foreshadows even more devastating judgment from a divinely commanded army. Their terrorizing powers compare only to those of the beast (Chapter 13). These infernal monsters attack only the wicked, not the saints. The wicked suffer even in this life as a preview of their final punishment.'[22]

OTHER INTERPRETATIONS OF THE LOCUSTS

The Idealist Redemptive view would say the vision depicts the self-defeating and tormenting nature of demonic wickedness that affects the human soul. Powers from the abyss do not attack the saints, only the wicked.

There are some historicists who wrongly see this as a depiction of the influence of Islam on a largely degenerate and unspiritual world.

The futurists believe it will be an unleashing of demonic spirits loosed on the earth shortly before Jesus's return.

There have even been interpretations that suggest this is a reference to helicopter warfare. It would not be helpful either to speculate or to find a specific interpretation. What we can understand is that the fallen star (probably Satan himself), had been given the key to the bottomless pit and all his ferocity has been loosed on the earth with a host of demons. These demons have an arch-demon called Abaddon or Apollyon.

We need to remember that Satan is not omnipresent, so this host of demons are loosed to carry out his evil assignments against humanity.

In spite of all these judgments, mankind still does not repent. Revelation 9:20-21 (NKJV) says:

'But the rest of mankind, who were not killed by these plagues, did not repent of the works of their hands, that they should not worship demons, and idols of gold, silver, brass, stone and wood, which can neither see nor hear nor walk. And they did not repent of their murders or their sorceries or their sexual immorality or their thefts.'

The implication here is that there were false teachers and it also fits with Romans 1 where worship of the creature and creation rather than the Creator brings judgment.

Idolatry can include materialism, sport, careers and leisure activities, and although there is nothing intrinsically wrong with these things, when they dominate life and leave no room for God, they become idolatrous.

Next we get a sub-plot before the sounding of the seventh trumpet, which will herald the end of the act.

THE INTERLUDE BETWEEN THE SIXTH AND SEVENTH TRUMPETS

A sub-plot is revealed.

Before the seventh trumpet sounds at the end of chapter 11, there are two other incidents recorded in the vision that form an interlude between the sixth and seventh trumpets.

In chapter 10, John hears a loud voice like seven thunders. The description of the angelic figure that appears can only apply to Jesus himself.

John is about to write what he hears the voice saying but he is told not to do that and seal up the book. It reminds us of Paul recounting how a man in Christ was taken up into a third heaven and not being permitted to tell what he saw. There is a lesson here for us to be careful when we make pronouncements about what we feel God is showing us. Sometimes it is better to stay quiet. Recently there have been prophetic words by known, established prophets that have proved to be incorrect. We always need to be sure about saying what God says, and not to speak flippantly.

John was then told by the angel (Jesus) to take the scroll or little book and eat it. When he does this, it is as sweet as honey in his mouth but becomes bitter in his stomach as he digests it.

This speaks of the dichotomy of God's word. When God speaks it is sweet to believers but bitter to unbelievers. It could also mean that the Word itself is sweet, but as we speak it out it brings judgment and an angry response hence the bitterness.

This book parallels the book with seven seals.

The book with seven seals speaks of Christ's rule over the earth and also of the inheritance for the church.

We are still awaiting the seventh trumpet as chapter 11 begins. John is given a measuring rod to measure the temple of God.

This again is a reference to the church. In Ephesians 2:21 Paul says that the church is being built into a holy temple, the dwelling place of God.

More symbolism regarding objects and time is included. The two lampstands and two olive trees are both symbols of the church and these two objects materialize into what are called the two witnesses. They are not named, but by their description we can identify them as Moses and Elijah. Futurists tend to believe that Moses and Elijah will actually appear in Jerusalem, be killed and then be raised to life. Alongside that belief the reference to 1,260 days and three and a half days, has provoked all kinds of weird and wonderful interpretations. However, it would seem that both of these amounts of time run parallel and both refer to the whole of the church age.

The two witnesses, Moses and Elijah, the two lampstands and the two olive trees all speak of the church. The idea of two witnesses is a principle that runs throughout Scripture and on the Mount of Transfiguration when Moses and Elijah appeared to Jesus, they were representing the Law and prophets of the Old Testament, confirming Jesus's deity and his mission.

Here they are representing the whole church. The fact that they are slain and then rise again in this vision could be a reference to the times when the church has made little impact on the world. The Dark Ages might be a case in point but even when the church has been at its lowest, God has always resurrected it. We would do well not to try and be over-literal and specific about this but see the glory of a resurrected, victorious church in action before the seventh trumpet sounds.

This great hymn of praise then erupts in Revelation 11:17 (NKJV):

'We give You thanks, O Lord God Almighty,
The One who is and who was and who is to come,
Because You have taken Your great power and reigned.'

As heaven opens, we get a glorious glimpse of our eternal destiny, with all the magnificence and wonder of being with God.

CHAPTER 9
HORRIBLE HISTORIES
Read Revelation 12 – 14

We now come to the visions and events recorded between chapters 12 and 14. These chapters introduce us to a third group of visions which reveal the histories of various characters who are involved in a massive cosmic conflict. The subject of spiritual warfare is usually related to what me might call 'deliverance ministry'. Approximately one third of Jesus's ministry on earth was taken up with the casting out of demons and he equipped the disciples and the 72 to go out on mission giving them the authority to cast out demons too. When they returned, they came back rejoicing because of their success. However, Jesus reminds them that their rejoicing should be over the fact that their names are written in heaven. He told them that he had seen Satan fall from heaven like lightning and now they had been given authority to tread on serpents and scorpions and over all the power of the enemy (Luke 10:17-20).

However, the subject of spiritual warfare is far greater than just the casting out of demons, and it is in the Book of Revelation that we learn that this kingdom activity in which the disciples were engaged is part of a much bigger picture of cosmic conflict.

In Revelation 12 we are introduced to a fearsome being, a great red dragon with seven heads and ten horns and with seven diadems on each head. We also meet a woman, the beast and the false prophet and again we encounter the number 1,260. (The meaning of the 1,260 days will be revealed in the following chapter.)

There are angels, the son of man and great pronouncements. All of these are involved in a massive cosmic conflict.

As we read the Scriptures from the start many Bible stories reveal the battle between good and evil. We see a strong enemy constantly seeking to thwart the plan of God and his people. The story of the Exodus from Egypt reveals a massive attack on the people of God by the Egyptian ruler, Pharaoh. The magicians of Egypt used their black arts to parody the signs and wonders performed by Moses, but in the end, God brought his people through a great deliverance. The story is well known.

In Revelation this conflict is explained so that the church can understand the nature of the battle and the completeness of the victory. As we unveil the different characters involved, we see each one's part and position in this heavenly war and how it affects the happenings on earth. The visions in the book now begin to intensify and at first reading may appear to be fanciful and speculative. However, as we understand the symbolism, we will be helped to understand how God protects his church and gives us victory. The battle is in the heavenly places but affects us here on earth.

Earlier, when we were considering the breaking of the seals, we noticed that spiritual forces are unleashed against believer and unbeliever alike, in accordance with the command of the resurrected Christ.

The sounding of the seven trumpets in paralleling the seals demonstrates God's judgment on hardened humanity. Throughout all this, God's people are spiritually protected.

Chapters 12 to 22 tell the same story as chapters 1 to 11 but in expanded detail, giving greater intensity to the events as history unfolds.

The evil one or Satan has already made an appearance in the earlier chapters. We saw Satan's throne at the church in Pergamum, and we see him again at the sounding of the fifth trumpet in chapter 9.

In these chapters we see Satan initiating the trials and persecution of the saints as he unleashes the beast and the false prophet. Babylon is also his servant. The four figures are the devil, the beast, the false prophet and the harlot (Babylon).

It is the devil who is behind this great manifestation of evil, but he can only attack within prescribed time periods as God, within his sovereignty, allows. But, behind every attack is the devil or Satan.

Dr Martyn Lloyd-Jones preached a series of sermons on Ephesians 6 which became the basis for his book *The Christian Warfare*. He says:

'It is my belief, as I have tried to show in my exposition of the apostles' warnings, that the modern world, and especially the history of the present century, can only be understood in terms of the unusual activity of the devil and the "principalities and powers" of darkness. Indeed, I suggest that a belief in a personal devil and demon activities is the touchstone by which one can most easily test any profession of Christian faith today.

'I make no apology, therefore, for having considered the matter in such detail. It is essential for successful living of the Christian life, and for the peace and happiness and joy of the individual Christian, and also for the prosperity of the church in general.

'In a world of collapsing institutions, moral chaos, and increasing violence, never was it more important to trace the hand of the "prince of the power of the air, the spirit that now worketh in the children of disobedience" and then not only learn how to wrestle with him and his forces, but also how to overcome them by "the blood of the Lamb and the word of our testimony." If we cannot discern the chief cause of our ills, how can we hope to cure them?'[23]

Those words, first published in 1976, are as relevant today and we can add to them the recent histories of wars, the refugee crisis, disease, mental health issues, family breakdown, violence and an upsurge in gross immorality.

The Book of Revelation could be no more relevant in its outlining of the conflict between good and evil, than in our present age.

The way to interpret the Book of Revelation is from Scripture itself and so its references to the devil, Satan, and the red dragon need to be understood in the light of other Scriptures about him.

NAMES OF SATAN

Satan has several names.

1. He is called a son of God (meaning he is a created being).
2. Satan, meaning accuser, slanderer (1 Samuel 29:4, 1 Kings 11:14, Zechariah 3:1).
3. Tempter (Matthew 4:3, 1 Thessalonians 3:5).
4. Dragon and Serpent (Revelation 12:9).
5. Destroyer (Revelation 9:11).
6. Prince of the power of the air (Ephesians 2:2).
7. Belial/Beelzebub (2 Corinthians 6:15, Matthew 12:27, Luke 11:15).
8. Ruler of this world (John 12:31, John 14:30, John 16:11, 2 Corinthians 4:4).
9. The evil one (when we pray 'deliver us from evil' in the Lord's prayer it actually means deliver us from the evil one; evil does not exist as an abstract concept).

CHARACTERISTICS OF SATAN

He is:

1. Bound (Mark 3:27, Revelation 20:2).
2. Cunning, with power (Genesis 3:1, Acts 26:18).
3. Violent (Mark 5:3, Luke 4:35, Matthew 11:12).
4. Deceitful (Luke 22:3, John 13:27, Acts 5:3, Acts 13:10).

5. Dominating (Revelation 2:13).
6. Persistent (Mark 15:30, Revelation 12).
7. Cowardly (James 4:7).

The Book of Revelation reveals the battle between God and the devil, but it is a battle that has been won already. The result, right from the beginning when Satan rebelled, was never in doubt. It is important to remember that the devil has none of God's attributes and so he is not omnipresent. He has an evil hierarchy that carries out his assignments and in Ephesians chapter 6:10-20 where Paul writes about spiritual warfare and our need as the church and as individuals to be clothed in the armour of God, he refers to a hierarchy in the world of evil spirits. There are thrones, dominions, rulers and authorities all conspiring to threaten and undermine the working of God.

Before Jesus began his public ministry on earth, he had a confrontation with the evil one and was tempted in the same way as Adam (Matthew 4:1-11). The root of the temptation was the lust of the eyes, the lust of the flesh and the pride of life. Adam saw the tree and that the fruit was good. The three temptations Jesus faced had the same elements as the ones Adam faced and in which he failed.

Jesus was tempted to satisfy his flesh by turning the stones into bread. He was tempted by pride when Satan tried to entice him to jump from the pinnacle of the temple to receive public acclaim. He was tempted by the lust of the eyes when Satan showed him all the kingdoms of this world, declaring they would be his if he would just bow down and bring worship to Satan.

The kingdoms of the world were not his to offer but he still sought to draw Jesus into something that would destroy his mission. Jesus was totally unyielding to the temptations which the first Adam had failed to resist.

It is no wonder that Jesus the man, the second Adam, was able to defeat the emissaries of his adversary, the demonic hordes that had enslaved the people he came to redeem.

When Jesus announced the Great Commission before he ascended, his followers were charged not only to heal the sick but also to cast out demons. The early chapters of Acts show us they were able to fulfil and continue that ministry.

The Book of Revelation shows us that there is an incredible amount of demonic activity, and as we read this book it should provoke us to see that the Great Commission has not changed. Through the power of the cross, the resurrection and the exaltation of Jesus and because the Holy Spirit has been poured out, we have the authority to continue what Jesus demonstrated. Revelation should encourage us to pursue ministering to bring deliverance to those ensnared by demonic powers.

It is the Great Commission and if we are not doing it, we are not fulfilling it.

The horrible histories of spiritual warfare show us we are in a battle where we wrestle, not against flesh and blood, but against this evil hierarchy of the demonic world. Revelation exposes it and encourages us that the victory is won.

CHAPTER 10
SEVEN VISIONS
Read Revelation 12 – 15

THE FIRST VISION

Before the red dragon is unleashed, Revelation chapter 12 begins with a 'sign appeared in heaven: a woman clothed with the sun, with the moon under her feet and on her head a crown with twelve stars' (ESV). We are told that she is pregnant and about to give birth. It is then that we get the appearance of the red dragon, and his opposition to the woman and his desire to devour her child.

She gives birth to a male child, who we are told is to rule the nations with a rod of iron, and her child is caught up to God and his throne.

After this the woman flees into the wilderness to a place prepared for her by God, so that she will be nourished for 1,260 days.

There has been much debate over many years by various commentators as to who this woman actually represents. There have been strong arguments for her representing the nation of Israel. The sun and moon, and the reference to the 12 stars could be a reference to Joseph's dream and the prophetic nature of that dream being fulfilled in the nation of Israel.

There are others who would say it is a reference to Mary, the mother of Jesus, and yet others who would say it is a reference to the church.

It would seem logical that this vision of the woman incorporates all three perspectives, representing the faithful community of believers of all ages including Israel. The symbolism speaks of the preservation and protection of God and his purpose for his people. Through each age the dragon has done everything he can to attack and destroy God's purpose. Old Testament Israel was constantly under attack and events like the Babylonian captivity and exile reveal a very low point in Israel's history. In the period between the Old and New Testaments, where the prophetic voice is silent, there were many attacks on the nation, ending ultimately with the Roman occupation. Where were the promises of God in that period?

God's plan could not be thwarted. Israel, often described as a bride and even as an unfaithful wife, is the nation that produces the Messiah. So, this woman could refer to the nation of Israel.

However, the description and feel of this vision could so easily apply to Mary the mother of Jesus, and the fact that she gave birth in such painful and difficult circumstances. We have romanticized the Christmas story, but the facts of the matter show that everything conspired not only to make this birth as difficult as possible, but even the baby's own life was threatened. Herod tried to kill him.

The fact that the child born to the woman is the Messiah cannot be doubted. His ruling of the nations with a rod of iron fulfils the prophecy of the Messianic Psalm 2:2,7-9.

'The kings of the earth take their stand, and the rulers take counsel together against the LORD and against His Anointed . . . "I will surely tell of the decree of the LORD: He said to Me, 'You are My Son, today I have begotten You. Ask of me, and I will surely give the nations as Your inheritance, and the very ends of the earth as Your possession. You shall break them with a rod of iron, You shall shatter them like earthenware.'"' (NASB)

There is a reference to the resurrection and ascension as this child was caught up to God and his throne. This is history compressed into one sentence, which gives the vision both impact and pace and hints at a fuller understanding of this victory to be revealed later. Satan opposes, God protects. (We need to remember that for ourselves, because we are in Christ.)

But the interpretation of this part of the vision does not end there. We are told that the woman fled into the wilderness where she had a place prepared for her by God for 1,260 days. This must surely be a reference to the church. The wilderness was often seen in the Old Testament as a place of God's protection of his people. It was in the wilderness that God protected them from Pharaoh and where he revealed his plans and purposes to them, in spite of their grumblings and murmurings. He still cared for them and protected them. David, Elijah, John the Baptist and Jesus himself all spent time in the wilderness. It would have been a place of both conflict and protection. The 1,260 days is always symbolic of the time between the ascension and the Second Coming in Revelation, so the implication here is that during the church age she is protected.

Dr David Campbell says,

'The 1,260 days = the 42 years of Israel in the desert = 42 encampments = 42 months of Elijah's time in the desert, remembering the church, or the covenant people are represented by the law and the prophets, Moses and Elijah. This makes sense of the 1,260 / 42 month references. The wilderness represents the church age between the deliverance from spiritual Egypt and arrival in the promised land, the New Jerusalem. This is why Revelation represents the church age as a second Exodus.'[24]

That the woman represents the church can be seen in many of the Old Testament prophecies where God's people are referred to as the daughter of Zion, and the prophecy of Isaiah 62:4-5 regarding the church is one of those. This great prophecy regarding Zion refers to the people of God as married, saying: 'For the Lord delights in you . . . For as a young man marries a virgin, so your sons will marry you; and as the bridegroom rejoices over the bride, so your God will rejoice over you' (NKJV).

It is significant that during the move of the Spirit in the Seventies, as the church was waking up to the fact that God wanted to restore many things the church had lost, we began to rediscover the gifts of the Spirit, spiritual authority, biblical church government, community and body life that reflected something of the church in the New Testament. Many of our worship songs declared prophetically what God was saying and Isaiah 62 was a great source of lyrics for songwriters. What God is doing in his church today is the ongoing fulfilment of the 'woman in the wilderness'. It is incredible how biblical imagery is connected throughout the whole of the Bible.

The second part of this vision describes war in heaven where the archangel Michael and his angels wage war on the dragon and his angels.

The dragon and his angels could not defeat Michael and his angels. It says in Revelation 12:8-9: 'There was no longer a place found for them in heaven. And the great dragon was thrown down, the serpent of old who is called the devil and Satan, who deceives the whole world; he was thrown down to the earth, and his angels were thrown down with him' (NASB).

This is a description of the victory over Satan through the cross and the resurrection.

In the history of the world from the dawn of time to the Second Coming of Jesus there has always been this cosmic conflict and there have been various stages to the ultimate defeat of Satan.

The imagery of the dragon is seen throughout the Old Testament as the people of God were persecuted by evil nations, in whom the dragon worked his evil intentions. Such monsters as sea dragons and Leviathan are descriptions of Satanic activity.

THE ORIGIN OF THIS EVIL

There are two passages of Scripture, one in Isaiah 14:12-21 the other in Ezekiel 28, that describe a pre-cosmic fall where Lucifer, a magnificent and beautiful angel, got puffed up with pride and aspired to be like God. His rebellion took many from the angelic host and he was removed from the glory of God's presence.

In the passage in Ezekiel 28:1-10 the King of Tyre is shown to be a human king, puffed up with pride with a sense of his own importance. However, the prophecy takes on an allegorical dimension when Ezekiel says, 'Thus says the Lord God, "You had the seal of perfection, full of wisdom and perfect in beauty. You were in Eden, the garden of God."' (Ezekiel 28:12-13 NASB). The King of Tyre was never in Eden, so this confirms the allegorical, prophetic nature of this passage in describing Satan. There are some who have suggested that the allegory concerns Adam and this is a description of the effect of the fall on mankind. Whichever view we may hold, Satan is a created being who originally was an angel of light who rebelled against God.

2 Peter 2:4 makes reference to this when it says: 'For if God did not spare angels when they sinned but cast them into hell and committed them to pits of darkness reserved for judgment' (NASB). The verse then goes on to describe some Old Testament incidents showing the historical context of this. In the Old Testament Satan was active, and this culminates in the temptations of Jesus in the Gospels. It is likely that Jesus's description of Satan's fall from heaven in Luke 10:18 is referring to this banishing from the presence of God pre the fall of Adam. The fact that Job 1:6 witnesses an appearance of Satan while the court of heaven is in session shows that he had a sphere of activity.

VICTORY OVER EVIL

This vision in Revelation 12 is a further stage in Satan's defeat. The death and resurrection of Jesus have brought about a conclusive victory over Satan and his demonic powers, a victory in which the church become participants.

The hymn of praise that rises over the defeat of Satan now echoes down the centuries, and we do not just sing the hymn, we can enjoy the victory.

Revelation 12:10-11 says:

'Now the salvation, and the power, and the kingdom of our God and the authority of His Christ have come, for the accuser of our brethren has been thrown down, he who accuses them before our God day and night. And they overcame him because of the blood of the Lamb and because of the word of their testimony, and they did not love their life even when faced with death.' (NASB)

There have been many books written, counselling programmes and techniques explored, and sermons preached on living in victory. Throughout my years in ministry I have counselled Christians who have not been living in freedom. Sometimes there has been slavery to habits and addictions, and others have been affected by abuse, fear and rejection. Emotional damage can rob people of the inheritance of joy and peace in the Holy Spirit. Alongside this there can be demonic strongholds through occult involvement, curses, and generational sins that can hold people in captivity.

Whether it is healing from emotional pain, addictions or demonic bondage, God wants his people to be free. Revelation 12:11 gives us some keys to unlock them, whether we are praying for inner healing or breaking strongholds caused by demons.

The first thing we see in this verse is that we overcome by the blood of the Lamb. The blood of Jesus is foreshadowed in the Old Testament. The foreshadowing is explained in Hebrews 9:7: 'The high priest enters once a year, not without taking blood, which he offers for himself and the sins of the people committed in ignorance' (NASB). Entrance into the presence of God could only be gained by the shedding of blood as a sacrifice for the sins of the people. Sin brings about death, so the death and blood sacrifice appease a holy God. The old covenant with its laws, rituals and sacrifices were fulfilled in Jesus who died and shed his blood, so that under the new covenant we all have free access into God's presence.

In the New Testament, the blood of Christ is frequently referred to. Our sins are forgiven, we have redemption, we are made clean from all our sins: past, present and future.

It is the blood that helps us in our relationships with one another. 1 John 1:7 says: 'If we walk in the Light as He Himself is in the Light, we have fellowship one with another, and the blood of Jesus His Son cleanses us from all sin' (NASB).

Our sin prevents access to God but the shed blood of Jesus changes things. The writer to the Hebrews calls this a new and living way (Hebrews 10:19-20).

This was prefigured in the Book of Exodus when the children of Israel were delivered from Egypt. The blood of the lamb placed on their doorframes meant that the angel of death would pass over that household. The story is well known and was integral to the life of Israel as they annually celebrated the feast of Passover.

It was at this feast that Jesus instituted the Last Supper, with bread representing his body and the wine his blood.

Jesus the Lamb shed his blood on the cross fulfilling all the demands of the old covenant.

The blood of God's son means he passes over our sinfulness, he forgives and cleanses.

Another verse which helps us understand the power and effectiveness of Jesus's blood is 1 Peter 1:18-19: 'You were not redeemed with perishable things like silver or gold from your futile way of life inherited from your forefathers, but with the precious blood, as of a lamb unblemished and spotless, the blood of Christ' (NASB).

The blood of Jesus deals with the fact that we were born in sin, which is passed from one generation to another. We are redeemed from the curse of Adam.

I have also found this verse powerful when I have prayed for people who are under the curse of generational sin. Over the years in counselling and pastoral situations I have encountered demonic strongholds over families where repeated problems have dominated. I have found it very effective to break family curses on the basis of this verse. There are many testimonies that could be shared of people now living in freedom.

Our position in Christ is now one of total freedom from every past sin so the enemy has no grounds to bring his accusations. We have clean consciences because of the blood.

I have sometimes heard expressions like 'pleading the blood' and 'placing the blood on our lives' and even placing the blood on such objects as a car, to prevent accidents.

Such ideas can become 'mantra-like' and verge on the superstitious.

To overcome by the blood of the Lamb is to declare what God's word says the blood does.

The Father sees the blood and declares us forgiven and free.

These great truths are expressed clearly in the hymn 'Before the Throne of God Above' by Charitie Lees Bancroft (1841–1892). The final verse says:

Behold him there the risen Lamb
My perfect spotless righteousness
The great unchangeable I am.

The king of glory and of grace.
One with himself I cannot die,
My soul is purchased with his blood.
My life is hid with Christ on high.
With Christ my Saviour and my God.
(Copyright © 1997 Sovereign Grace Worship)[25]

Another way in which we overcome is 'by the word of our testimony'. There is power in declaring Scripture, not by speaking out random texts, but by absorbing into our lives the truth of God's word. We should study it, meditate on it, and live out its teaching. There can be a danger that we live by subjective feelings rather than what God says. When Jesus was tempted by the devil in the wilderness, he answered the temptation with 'it is written' (Matthew 4:4).

I was once praying for someone who manifested a demon. The evil being holding this person captive started speaking through her saying: 'I am a lion. I am going to kill you.'

The person's face contorted and aggressively started to attack me. It was an uncomfortable situation, but a passage of Scripture immediately came to mind. It was the prophetic passage in Isaiah 35:8-9 where he talks about Zion's glorious future.

'A highway shall be there, and a road, and it shall be called the Highway of Holiness. The unclean shall not pass over it, but it shall be for others. Whoever walks the road, although a fool, shall not go astray. No lion shall be there, nor shall any ravenous beast go up on it.' (NKJV)

As I proclaimed this verse the demon left the person and they were freed.

We not only overcome by the blood of the Lamb and the word of God, but also by our full consecration to him.

The third part of the verse in Revelation 12:11 says: 'They did not love their life even when faced with death' (NASB).

The word 'consecration' is not often used today, but there is a call in the Christian life to the kind of consecration that withstands the taunts of the enemy, the mockery of others, persecution, and even death itself. There are many Christians in the world today who are living with the threat of martyrdom, and yet remaining true to Jesus and his word.

There is a huge challenge to the church today to stand out against inverted moral values where biblical issues on morality are opposed and termed intolerant.

The Book of Revelation reveals the intensity of the spiritual battle, but Jesus has defeated Satan. We are called to stand in that victory as we overcome by the blood of the Lamb, the word of our testimony and live lives fully consecrated to God.

In 1982 I experienced a time of intense spiritual warfare, and saw many people released from demonic bondage. I was in meetings where there were many outbursts of demonic activity. It was a powerful and exhausting time as many people were set free. After one particular meeting I went home and wrote the song 'O Lamb of God'.

O Lamb of God, you take away our sin
You clothe us now in robes of righteousness.
You set us free and protect us from all harm.
In holiness we worship you.
And we shall overcome, by the blood of the Lamb
As we declare the testimony of your word.
We shall overcome, by the blood of the Lamb

As we declare the word of God.

(Copyright © 1983 Thankyou Music)[26]

It became the theme song and album title for The Downs Bible Week in 1983.

It was written in the heat of the battle and its truth kept us focused on Jesus's victory for us.

This first vision concludes with the defeated dragon, still displaying some strength and persecuting the woman (the church).

However, we see the church protected as she is carried on the two wings of a great eagle into the wilderness (protection), where she is cared for throughout the whole of the church age (time and times and half a time).

Satan the dragon is still active and seeks to drown the woman in a flooding river. However, the earth opens its mouth (metaphorically), and swallows up the flood.

Isaiah 59:19 says: 'When the enemy comes in like a flood, the Spirit of the LORD will lift up a standard against him' (NKJV).

The final verses of this first vision should inspire us to stand in the victory, and as the enemy spews out his worst, to remember that the spirit of the Lord lifts up a standard against him. It is no coincidence that Isaiah 59 is the passage on which Paul bases his teaching on spiritual warfare in Ephesians 6, about the whole armour of God. Isaiah 59 describes God rousing himself and putting on his own armour. He puts on righteousness as a breastplate and the helmet of salvation on his head. This is the armour in which we are clothed.

Victory is ours. We overcome. We are not only able to stand against the dragon's accusations, but we can thwart his activity as he spews out his rivers of violence and hatred. The Spirit of the Lord lifts up a standard against him. Jesus said: 'I will build my church, and the gates of hell shall not prevail against it' (Matthew 16:18 ESV).

The victory over Satan and our identification with that victory leads us to the next vision.

THE SECOND VISION (Revelation 13:1-10)

We now come to visions which cause the literalists to become more speculative than ever. The first half of chapter 13 introduces us to the beast and the second half of the chapter, which is the third vision in this sequence of visions, introduces us to the false prophet.

There are many different opinions as to what this chapter means and to whom it is referring. It is very important not to be either dogmatic or speculative, but to try and find the essence of what these visions teach us and their application for the church today.

The red dragon is clearly identified as Satan, but here we have Satan releasing another beast with seven heads inscribed with blasphemous names and ten horns with diadems. The beast has a ferocious look about him, looking like a leopard with the feet of a bear and the mouth of a lion. These are symbols of both power and savagery. The dragon gives this beast authority and power. One of the heads has a wound as if he had been slain but paradoxically the wound is healed. This beast is definitely against God and the people of God. He is given authority by the dragon to make war on the saints.

THE THIRD VISION (Revelation 13:11-18)

We now see another beast, this time arising from the earth with two horns and he spoke as a dragon.

There seems to be a spiritual power that he has as he performs signs and wonders which deceive humanity. His role is to get people to worship the beast and bring their allegiance to him.

He gives everyone a mark, without which people will be unable to buy or sell and who do not understand his number 666.

We need to take these two visions together to get the full impact of what they mean.

It would seem that the dragon, the beast from the sea, and the beast from the earth is a parody of the trinity. The beast, sometimes called the Antichrist (from John's epistle), or the man of lawlessness (from 2 Thessalonians 2:3) is a demonic counterpart to Christ. It is the dragon who gives him authority, and the fact that he has a fatal wound that is healed speaks of an apparent resurrection. He is given authority to infiltrate the world of government, the economy, and the whole fabric of society. There have been many who have sought to identify who this person is over the centuries. Despotic rulers have emerged and been named from Nero to Hitler and, in many ways, they qualify.

The big question is will there be an actual Antichrist, who could be identified as the beast. It would seem that this beast figure has been present throughout the church age in one form or another. Many speculative guesses have been made.

If the beast or Antichrist is a parody of Christ it would be logical to assume, that just as Christ has a body on earth, the church, so the beast is an evil spiritual being who has infiltrated governments and created a following. The absolute secularization of our world today is a possible example of this. When we use the term anti-Christ the word 'anti' actually means 'instead of' rather than 'against'.

It is possible that the beast, the Antichrist, the man of lawlessness, rather than being a specific person, is a spirit which works in a corporate fashion to reject the gospel. When the gospel is rejected, humanism replaces the worship of God and the dichotomy of exalting humanity, yet aborting babies, destroying the concept of family, sexual licence, the rich and poor divide, racial prejudice, authoritarianism and so many other things show just how evil the beast, the Antichrist, actually is.

Having said this, just as Jesus is returning, we should at least consider the possibility of someone emerging on the world stage as a great leader, the coming of an Antichrist. The problem for us would be identifying who that was, and the mistakes of history would be made again. We are safer to see the reality of the Antichrist spirit working in our day and make sure we are in the good of being 'in Christ' the people of God.

The false prophet, the beast from the earth, as we have seen, is a manifestation of a corporate spirit that infiltrates the spiritual life of the world. Some have identified the false prophet as other religions, such as Islam. It is much more likely to be syncretic religion with false teachers infiltrating the church. The rise of spirituality in our day could be another manifestation. It is really important that the true church remains true to the Bible not in word only and by paying lip-service. Biblical truth carefully expounded with a strong theological base is the crying need for the church today. There is a passion for signs and wonders and the ministry of the miraculous, which is very much needed. However, there can be a danger that things can go off course and Gnosticism and spiritual elitism can creep in. There is a type of Gnosticism that is close to the truth, but new revelation that is not grounded in sound theology is at best misleading and at worst, close to heresy. Jesus is the head of his church and he is still pouring out his gifts and ministries. The warning for us is that we are to be true Bible-believing Christians, living by the whole gamut and revelation of Scripture. Signs, wonders and miracles will genuinely follow churches and believers who are not diverted from truth. The parody of the trinity of dragon, beast and false prophet is something the modern church needs to be aware of and this seems to be what the vision is saying.

The mark of the beast is not a microchip or the number on a credit card, or something in the coronavirus vaccine. Just as we are sealed with the spirit and have the indelible imprint of Christ in our lives, the opposite of that is that the mark of the beast is the indelible imprint of the sealing of life without God.

The number 666 is quite simply the number that represents life without God. It is the number for man.

THE FOURTH VISION

We can enjoy a breath of fresh air as we see the church at worship in the fourth vision (Revelation 14). Jesus the Lamb is at the centre as the 144,000 representing the whole church of God, bring their worship. The lives of the worshippers have been made clean through the blood of the Lamb.

Let's continue to be a worshipping church here on earth, singing our praise from hearts made clean, living under the protection of our loving Father, being borne on eagles' wings, filled with the Holy Spirit and looking forward to the great day of the return of Jesus.

THE FIFTH VISION

This vision introduces events that later become more detailed. The angel announces the fall of Babylon. This is after another angel, flying in what is called the mid-heaven (the realm of spiritual activity on earth), calls for the preaching of the gospel to every tribe, tongue and nation. This will happen before the final judgment. There is also a call to worship.

The vision speaks of final judgment, warning the wicked and encouraging the saints. It also declares the rest of those who have died in the Lord and are now in his presence.

THE SIXTH VISION

This is a sombre picture of the final judgment. The symbolism is vivid as the grain and grapes are harvested. The grim picture of blood flowing from the winepress of God's wrath should make us aware of the total holiness of God. The fact that once again there are four angels, keeps the consistency of the symbolism of four, meaning that these angels are reaping the whole earth.

THE SEVENTH VISION

This is the Christian's hope and expectation as we receive a vision described as 'great and marvellous' in Revelation 15.

As this triumphant song of praise and worship rises, we as the church can join in with faith and joy, fixing our gaze on our eternal hope:

> *'Great and marvellous are Your works,*
> *O Lord God, the Almighty;*
> *Righteous and true are Your ways,*
> *King of the nations!*
> *Who will not fear, O Lord, and glorify Your name?*
> *For You alone are holy;*
> *For all the nations will come and worship before You,*
> *For Your righteous acts have been revealed.' (NASB)*

We end this section with our glorious hope of heaven, before we go back to another parallel set of sevens with the bowls of wrath.

So, let us keep our eyes on our heavenly end. In all the talk of judgment let's be thankful for the incredible mercy of our Father, the blood of the Lamb that saves us and the power of the Spirit who makes all this real for us.

CHAPTER 11
THE BOWLS OF WRATH
Read Revelation 16

We now come to another set of seven visions, the seven bowls of wrath. The mention of a concept like 'bowls of wrath' can instil a foreboding and make us not even want to consider it. This sevenfold vision parallels the seven seals, the seven trumpets and the seven visions we looked at in the previous chapter.

Here again we have an unfolding of the panorama of history, but the drama intensifies as the bowls are poured out.

Revelation 16:1 says: 'Then I heard a loud voice from the temple saying to the seven angels, "Go and pour out on the earth the seven bowls of the wrath of God"' (NASB).

Before we look at the content and context of these bowls, we need to look at the doctrinal and theological issues surrounding the wrath of God. This is not a subject that is preached on very often in today's church, but that has not always been the case. When I grew up in the 1950s, evangelistic preaching frequently focused on people being exhorted to escape the horrors of hell. Fire and brimstone were popular images especially from evangelists. The Victorian era would have been a time when the concept of the stern father and family discipline were commonplace. This continued into the twentieth century. (I know I am generalizing, but it was a trend.)

In today's church, even amongst the keenest of evangelicals, the belief in God's wrath and eternal punishment may be there in the mind because we know it is in the Bible, but it is rarely talked or preached about. The emphasis on God's love meeting human need, giving us identity, inward security and a sense of purpose in life have been more socially acceptable themes on which to major. A gospel that satisfies human need and heals the body through the ministry of signs and wonders, is a far more attractive proposition than telling people that if they don't repent, they will go to hell.

In the eighteenth century the revivalist Jonathan Edwards preached a very powerful sermon, 'Sinners in the hands of an angry God'. It brought about a great revival with people reportedly clinging to the pillars of the church for fear of being transported to hell in that very moment. I'm not sure that kind of preaching would go down well in today's culture. The prevailing thinking is motivation by love and grace rather than fear. However, we must ask the question, have we abandoned an important aspect of biblical teaching?

My education in the Fifties was very much based on fear of the teacher, and in the first secondary school I attended every teacher taught with a cane in their hand. During the mid- Sixties when I trained as a teacher, the emphasis had moved away from education through fear to education through motivation and creating a hunger and thirst for knowledge. Educational philosophy became child-centred, endorsing the significance and freedom of the human spirit. Of course, this was a far better way to educate, but has this liberalism gone too far? Gradually the concept of punishment is being eradicated from the family, education and perhaps even from society itself. It would be a totally retrograde step to go back to how things were but is there a danger of so emphasizing individualism and freedom that parameters of accountability and consequences for our actions are no longer deemed necessary? I would dare to ask the question of preachers and contemporary theologians: are we too influenced by our cultural liberalism?

I am asking the question of myself because I have struggled to know how to explain these bowls of wrath. Is this a step too far in understanding a God of love?

Before we can answer this question, we need to take a step back and look at what God has revealed about himself in the Bible. In doing this, one mistake we can make is to think that the God of the Old Testament acted differently from the God of the New Testament. In the Old Testament we see the love, compassion and mercy of God, as well as his wrath and judgments. In the New Testament we see the wrath and judgment of God as well as his love, mercy and grace. Of course, 'mercy triumphs over judgment' and judgment in Isaiah 28:21 is described as 'his strange work' (KJV).

In his book *Systematic Theology*, Robert Letham puts it like this:

'ABSOLUTE attributes are those without which God would not be God; infinity, eternity, spirituality, omnipotence, omniscience and omnipresence are intrinsic to God Himself.

'RELATIVE attributes are those involved in God's relationship to the creation: He is holy, patient, merciful, creator, and preserver.

'Some attributes are related purely to sin: wrath is a prime example. Apart from human sin, God would not exercise wrath, for there would be nothing about which to be wrathful. However, once he had created humanity, Adam disobeyed his law, with the consequent devastating effects on the human race and the cosmos itself, God, being righteous and holy himself, reacted with settled hostility to the emergence of rebellion in his prime creature. This was no change in God; it was the creature that had changed.

'Mercy is an outflow of his goodness. Since he is eternally good in relation to his creatures, he displays his goodness in showing mercy and grace to them. So too, holiness and wrath are the responses of God's inherent goodness to the existence and the sin of the creature.'[27]

To confine the wrath of God to the Old Testament is to deny his character. It is in the Book of Romans, which is the key New Testament book to explain both the theology and experience of salvation, that we get the concept of God's wrath mentioned at least ten times. Paul was not ashamed to preach it. We shouldn't be ashamed to preach it either. In Romans 1 where we get the devastating effects of the fall upon the human race, Paul's unfolding of God's plan of redemption begins with the wrath of God. Romans 1:18 says: 'For the wrath of God is revealed ['*apokalupsis*'] from heaven against all ungodliness and unrighteousness of men, who suppress the truth in unrighteousness' (NKJV).

Paul then goes on to outline the devastating effects of the fall on humanity.

In the earlier chapter on judgment we considered the creation being 'out of joint', showing us that the judgments of God are continuously unfolding. When we understand this, we can understand the bowls of wrath.

The fact that these are bowls of wrath connects with the prayers of the saints which have been gathered up previously like incense.

As the church prays, so God acts. It is important to keep praying so we get God's perspective on what is happening in the world. As terrible calamities and disasters happen in the world it should be a reminder that God is still in control and working out his plan. Yes, we do all we can to alleviate suffering and not stand idly by with a fatalistic attitude. We work to see the kingdom come, even in the devastations that happen, but we work and pray with the confident assurance that God will ultimately work out his purpose.

Notice that the chapter begins with a loud voice in the temple, the place of God's presence, where he hears and answers prayer. In Revelation 16:7 there is a cry from under the altar, the place where the prayers of the martyrs and saints have been gathered up and are now being answered.

As we see these bowls poured out it should remind us that Scripture is its own best commentary. Many, especially the literalists, have come up with speculative interpretations of what these bowls mean and tried to interpret them through contemporary events. These bowls of wrath are reminders of the deliverance from Egypt and the plagues that hardened Pharaoh's heart. The lesson we learn from this is that just as Pharaoh's kingdom collapsed after the plagues and the deliverance through the Red Sea, so the day will come when the world systems will collapse at the coming of Jesus. The plagues in Exodus foreshadow what is happening through the church age, during the great cosmic conflict.

What the trumpets have stated, the bowls are now developing even further, and not just with warnings but with the actions that the warnings had predicted. The trumpet visions are sketches of what will happen, whereas the bowls give the full picture. We do need to remember that these outpourings of judgments are on the unbelieving world systems. We who are in Christ are protected. We may be affected by world events, but we are safe and secure in Christ even if we suffer or are martyred.

FIRST BOWL

A loathsome and malignant sore is poured out on the people who had the mark of the beast. Remember the plague in Egypt where the people were covered in boils? This clearly represents the presence of physical disease.

SECOND BOWL

The second bowl parallels the second trumpet but with an even greater level of devastation. It is a reflection of the plague in Exodus 7 where Moses turns the Nile into blood. The idea here seems to suggest economic disaster. The sea is often used to express the idea of maritime trade and prosperity. G.K. Beale suggests that this is yet more imagery suggesting human loss of life as well as the idea of trade and commerce being affected. It is also consistent with the sea imagery in Revelation bearing a negative idea.

THIRD BOWL

The rivers and springs turn to blood. This is a reminder of the Nile in Egypt being turned to blood. Both the second and third bowl speak of the world's economic system being affected and of regional and global disasters in trade and commerce. There have been reports of some of the major rivers of the world, including the Nile, being polluted through plastic waste.

FOURTH BOWL

This shows the world being scorched with fire and heat. This could speak of natural and of ecological disasters. We are reminded of the hail and fire which struck the Egyptians.

FIFTH BOWL

This darkness speaks of the upsetting of worldly governments. The throne of the beast is affected and things in which people have put their trust such as wealth, riches and ungodly governments. People will be in despair because they have believed lies. The breakdown of morality is due to the fact that people have believed lies about sexuality, marriage, abortion, the value of human life and anything else that has challenged biblical morality and how humans should behave. Even after this there is still no repentance.

SIXTH BOWL

We are now heading towards the final judgment of the world as we know it. This vision has three distinctive parts. The first is of the river

Euphrates drying up to prepare the way for the kings from the East. In the Old Testament, when King Cyrus defeated Babylon so the Jews could go back to their homeland, he dammed the river Euphrates so his troops could gain access to the city. Cyrus had come from the East to defeat the Babylonians. God used this pagan king to bring judgment and see the nation of Israel released from captivity. The drying up of water and riverbeds is an image that occurs frequently in Old Testament prophecy, speaking of God's judgment. John gives a universal application to the mention of the drying up of the river Euphrates, as Babylon symbolizes the structures, values and economics of a world system in the hands of the beast, which has no time for God. The drying up of the Euphrates is the symbolic beginning of the destruction of contemporary spiritual Babylon.

In Revelation 17:1, Babylon, here called the 'great harlot' (NKJV), is said to sit on many waters. The imagery of sea, river and waters elsewhere in the book suggests figuratively that this reference to the Euphrates drying up is a picture of something more universal than just one geographical place. The reference in 17:1 speaks of multitudes of tribes and languages.

The reference to the kings of the East is clarified in verse 14 as kings of the whole world, hence not referring to a Middle Eastern end-times conflict. It speaks of rulers from across the whole world acting under the demonic influence of the beast (but still under God's sovereign control), to bring down Babylon.

The next part of the vision, from the pouring out of the sixth bowl of wrath in Revelation 16:12-13 describes three frogs, described as demonic spirits, coming out of the mouths of the dragon, the beast and the false prophet. Frogs were unclean animals and connected with a powerful Egyptian deity. This speaks of a releasing of demonic influence into the world. The performing of false signs, wonders and miracles will be deceptive. It is difficult to speculate what these signs, wonders and miracles will be, but some part at least of its outworking could be in the realm of the world's economy where it could look as though there is a massive recovery, and a false sense of well-being is created. We do not know exactly, and speculation would not be helpful, but what we do know is that there will be a massive demonic onslaught released into the world. The fact that these spirits are described as unclean is interesting. The Greek word is '*porneia*', a word associated with immorality. Sexual exploitation and all kinds of depravity will be evident. The imagery of frogs is often seen in the Old Testament prophetic writings to symbolize the demonic.

The final part of the vision from the sixth bowl reveals there will be a great gathering for a final war. Many Old Testament prophecies speak of a gathering of nations against the people of God. We now come to an idea that has provoked many speculative interpretations over the centuries of the church age.

Revelation 16:16 says: 'And they gathered them together to the place which in Hebrew is called Har-Magedon' (NASB).

The concept of the 'battle of Armageddon' has often been used in descriptions of fierce battles in the history of warfare. For example, the Battle of the Somme in World War I.

H.G. Wells wrote a short story called *The Dream of Armageddon.*

Futurists believe the battle of Armageddon will take place in Israel as the armies of the world confront this small nation. This is equated with all sorts of speculative notions about the Temple being rebuilt. This interpretation has led to some Western nations making political decisions regarding the nation of Israel. It is very important for us to see the difference between political Israel, and the true spiritual Israel which is the church, both in the Old and New Testaments. It is in Romans chapters 9 to 11 that we get the New Testament perspective on Israel. There is nowhere in the Book of Revelation where such speculative notions are even hinted at.

So, we need to ask the question, what is the battle of Armageddon? In Jewish thought 'har' or 'mountain' was a reference to Mount

Carmel and Meggido. These were the scenes of two Old Testament battles. Both of these mountains were synonymous for victory over the forces of evil, for the Jewish people. The fact that Mount Carmel and Meggido are two separate places shows that the word is a symbolic representation of the battle between good and evil.

Har-Magedon or Armageddon, like Babylon and the Euphrates, are not specific geographical locations, but they are symbolic names for events and situations.

Armageddon is the name of the final battle in which all the forces of evil are gathered in a great world conflict. It is possible that Armageddon will be a global event and will usher in the outpouring of the final bowl.

SEVENTH BOWL

The outpouring from the seventh bowl begins with a cry from the throne in Revelation 16:17: 'It is done.' This reminds us of the cry of Jesus from the cross when he called out, 'It is finished' (John 19:30). This was a victory cry declaring the work of redemption was now accomplished. This was the inauguration of a new age, the age of the church, comprising of redeemed people from every tribe, tongue and nation. Satan had been defeated. Jesus's cry was not 'I am finished' but 'It is finished'.

Now this cry from the throne inaugurates a new era where the old world as it was, is now being destroyed in order to usher in the new heavens and earth.

The earthquake, the falling of the great cities, the cup of wine of God's fierce wrath and the great plague of hail all declare, in this cosmic shaking, that only that which is of the kingdom of God will remain.

The pouring out of the bowls of wrath is not an easy passage to expound. Even with the possibility of different interpretations in some of the detail, the fact of the matter is that God will end things as they are and as what they have become, because of the sinfulness of the human race. It will be cataclysmic and fearsome but the hope for Christians is that it will usher in a whole new age.

CHAPTER 12
THE BEAST AND THE HARLOT
Read Revelation 17 and 18

The next two chapters give us more detail about the events following the outpouring of the seventh bowl and should be seen as an integral part of this final outpouring of judgment.

We are now introduced to another symbolic figure, the great harlot, the scarlet woman. John describes her as an adulteress who has committed acts of immorality with the kings of the earth, who were made drunk with the wine of her immorality.

John is carried away into the wilderness, or desert. This probably signifies the idea of John standing back from events to look at things objectively, so he could gain the right perspective. We have already seen that the desert is not necessarily a negative place in which to be, but a place of protection and withdrawal from the hustle and bustle of life. A few years ago, I had the wonderful experience of being in Dubai for several weeks, helping the church that meets there. Dubai is a fascinating city, incredibly rich and a symbol of affluence in trade and commerce. The shopping malls were full of goods that were way out of my price league.

The opulence spoke of wealth and manmade genius. If ever there was a symbol of Babylon this was it. It was seductive, enjoyable and yet it challenged my spiritual values. It spoke of opulent secularism, money and the pride of man. To get a respite from the hustle and clamour of the city we were taken out one day into the desert. Miles and miles of sand, it provided a respite from the cacophony of traffic noise and the general speed and pace of city life. It gave us time to reflect and think. I can't help feeling there was something of this desert experience for John, to prepare him for what he was about to see in this vision.

He sees a woman sitting on a scarlet beast full of blasphemous names, having seven heads and ten horns. She is clothed in purple and adorned with gold and precious stones and pearls. In her hand she holds a gold cup full of abominations and the unclean features of her immorality. Revelation 17:5 says : 'On her forehead a name was written: "MYSTERY, BABYLON THE GREAT, THE MOTHER OF HARLOTS AND OF THE ABOMINATIONS OF THE EARTH"' (NKJV). John then goes on to see the woman drunk with the blood of the witnesses of Jesus.

This woman is clearly connected to the beast and the allusion to the seven heads, the ten horns, the seven kings and the seven mountains all speak of the rule and government of the Antichrist figure.

All this is symbolic of the systems and governments of this world as they relate together under the influence of the beast. The reference to the seven mountains is reminiscent of Rome and the reference to the ten horns and ten kings speaks of a conglomeration of governments in the world being ruled by a world view without any reference to God. The trade, economic systems, culture, entertainment, leisure, lifestyle and the morality are all totally secular. Babylon represents the world system, the kingdom of this world, which is in direct opposition to the kingdom of God. Babylon is not a geographical place.

In the Old Testament story of the building of the tower of Babel we see man in his pride exalting himself above God.

When God acts in judgment to destroy the tower, it is the forerunner of the events we are reading of here. It was also the place where the civilization of Babylon under Nebuchadnezzar had its heyday in the days of Daniel the prophet. That same Nebuchadnezzar sent the children of Israel into seventy years of captivity and exile.

This description of Babylon is all symbolism for the secular world.

It is interesting to note that a futurist and literalist interpretation of Revelation has been shown to be suspect in European history in the last fifty years. When what was called the 'Common Market' first appeared on the political scene in the Sixties it was actually called the 'Treaty of Rome' (the city with seven hills). As the number of European countries signing the treaty increased, there came a point when the literalists and futurists in churches were looking out for a tenth nation to join. This would have been seen as a fulfilment of this prophecy and a sign that the Second Coming was near. The fact that at the time of writing there are twenty-seven countries in the EU and there is still a certain amount of uncertainty regarding its future illustrates how not to interpret Revelation.

The second part of this vision, from Revelation 17:14, reveals the conflict of two kingdoms in the earth. The Bible has sometimes been described as a tale of two cities, Jerusalem and Babylon. It is certainly the story of the conflict between good and evil, darkness and light, the kingdom of God and the kingdom of Satan.

In 17:14 we read of the conflict between the two kingdoms, as the kingdom of Babylon through the harlot, the scarlet woman, driven by the beast, wages war against the Lamb. However, we are given the outcome of the war in verse 14 as it says: 'The Lamb will overcome them, for He is Lord of lords and King of kings; and those who are with Him are called, chosen, and faithful' (NKJV).

The chapter ends with the hint that the beast and the harlot are getting into conflict with each other.

It is interesting to note the parallel between the Old Testament Queen Jezebel and this description of the harlot Babylon. It is also interesting to note that the church in Thyatira was condemned for tolerating Jezebelic influence. This more than hints at the fact that this could refer to apostasy within the church as the church is influenced by the ungodliness of the temporal, secular world. The concept of the church and state together is unbiblical, and secular government and the church do not mix. Secular governments are always going to be tempted by the beast and the harlot. There will never be any such thing as a Christian state or Christian government. That does not mean that secular governments will never have a social or moral conscience, but secular humanism will never change the world. It is a good thing for Christians to be in the political world acting as salt and light and they should seek to implement true Christian values to make society function well. However, light and darkness will always exist. Changing laws on morality will never change the hearts of men and women, only the gospel of the kingdom of God can do that. So, while Christians should seek to bring justice and speak up about issues like poverty, inequality, racism and other major social issues, these problems will never be solved through political ideology. Capitalism, socialism, despotism and any other form of government are all manifestations of Babylon. That is why Jesus said there would be wars and rumours of wars and nation would rise against nation as different ideologies come into conflict.

Having said that, it is important to remember that God in his sovereign will raises up governments for the benefit of mankind. In his common grace to the human race God provides both blessing and restraint. Calvin said there were relics of God in fallen man, and that is true of human individuals as well as cultures and governments. Authorities should be prayed for and laws obeyed as we are exhorted in Romans 13 and 1 Timothy 2. But we also need to recognize that sometimes governments come under demonic control and there is suffering and persecution. There have been different phases of history and differing geographical locations where both have been evident.

Although Christians in governments do their best to make their countries better, the sinfulness of mankind means that ultimately it is all a manifestation of the beast-controlled harlot, Babylon. That is why we need to build the church to manifest the kingdom of God.

Revelation 17:18 describes the fall of Babylon and the collapse of its economic system, culture and social structure. It is a devastating and frightening picture of the collapse of civilization as we know it, before the final ending of all things and Jesus returns.

The challenge for the church is not to compromise. We are to be in the world but not influenced by it. There can be a danger that even in good Spirit-filled evangelical churches, worldliness can govern and influence what we do. We need to make sure that our finances, our morality and our methods of government are impeccable. There is a fine line between being totally relevant in our contemporary world in how we do things and compromising with worldly methods that exclude the Spirit of God.

We need to remember the fate of Babylon.

Revelation 18:21-23 states:

'Then a strong angel took up a stone like a great millstone and threw it into the sea, saying, "So will Babylon, the great city, be thrown down with violence and will not be found any longer. And the sound of harpists and musicians and flute-players and trumpeters will not be heard in you any longer; and no craftsmen of any craft will be found in you any longer; and the sound of a mill will not be heard in you any longer; and the light of a lamp will not shine in you any longer; and the voice of the bridegroom and bride will not be heard in you any longer; for your merchants were the great men of the earth, because all the nations were deceived."' (NASB)

The chapter ends with the blood of prophets and saints and all who have been slain on the earth left in the devastation of Babylon's destruction, showing the total opposition of Babylon to the kingdom of God.

We are now coming to the climax of world history and in the next chapter we will read about the actual return of Jesus.

After all this devastation and judgment, we will end on a positive note and say:

'Hallelujah! For the Lord our God, the Almighty, reigns.
Let us rejoice and be glad and give the glory to Him.'[28]

CHAPTER 13
THE ARRIVAL OF THE KING

Read Revelation 19

HIS GLORIOUS APPEARING

I was a student at the University of Sussex in the Sixties when the buildings, designed by the great architect of that era, Sir Basil Spence, were a showcase for contemporary architectural design and heralded a new dawn for further educational establishments to challenge the more traditional universities. The centre piece was the Meeting House, a circular building with oblong windows paned with glass of different colours. With the light shining through, the effect was stunning. The acoustics made live music a joy to experience. No amplification was needed, not even for speech.

This was the home of the university chaplaincy and was also a place for students to meet and discuss all kinds of topics, mainly left-wing political ideals, the arts and, of course, religion. I had the joy of being involved in several musical performances, but I was also appointed to be the musical director of the Meeting House choir, a chamber choir which performed for the regular Sunday morning, Anglican-style worship. I did not last long. One Sunday morning a dramatic hymn written by the great Charles Wesley, about the Second Coming of Jesus was on the order of service. I will quote the first verse in full.

Lo! he comes with clouds descending,
Once for favoured sinners slain;
Thousand, thousand saints attending
Swell the triumph of his train.
Hallelujah! Hallelujah!
God appears on earth to reign.[29]

The choir was well-rehearsed and during the service we sang the usual psalm and our well-polished anthem. A fairly innocuous sermon was preached and then the chaplain announced the last hymn.

He invited the congregation to stand and said, 'Please do not worry about the words of our final hymn. You must de-mythologize it in your mind as you sing it.' The choir included several evangelical Christians and along with them I nearly had an apoplexy of rage at such a crass and apostate remark. We sang the hymn that morning with a fervour as though the event was about to happen. My role as director of music for the Meeting House choir ended that morning. It is interesting to note that the motto of the University of Sussex is, 'Be still and know'. The quote ends there and the 'that I am God' has been omitted. If ever there has been an illustration of apostasy that we have been looking at in Revelation, here it is.

Although as evangelicals we would never claim to de-mythologize the Second Coming, we do need to dispel some very misinformed views and poor exegesis of Scripture. Having said that, there are different views surrounding some of the details around this event, and we will have to make up our own minds. The fact of the matter is, Jesus will come again. It will be a literal, physical, bodily return and all evangelicals would believe that. However, some of the teaching around the detail needs unpacking.

Revelation brings us the climactic events that will close history. As we have studied this book, we have seen an unfolding of the panorama of history, the seven seals, the seven trumpets, the seven visions and the seven bowls of wrath. Each facet has moved towards a final event without the details of the final event being fully explained. They have only been hinted at.

As the seventh bowl was poured out, we saw the doom of Babylon and the judgment of God on all the ungodly systems, philosophies and cultures. The graphic descriptions of Babylon's defeat now give way to the one who has brought about this glorious victory. The King of kings and Lord of lords is about to make his appearance. There are several parts to the scenes surrounding the actual appearance of Jesus and we must be careful not to try and construct a definitive timeline of the events. Centre stage is the glorious appearing of Jesus, but in the first six verses of Revelation 19 we also have a worshipping church, from verses 7-10 the marriage supper of the Lamb, from verses 11-16 the appearance of Jesus, and from verses 17-21 we have the judgment and doom of the beast, the false prophet and everything that has opposed God. This chapter is more of a collage of events, each one in our sight at the same time. However, we need to focus on each part so that we can then stand back, look at the whole, and get the full picture with understanding.

WORSHIP

The chapter begins with worship. Worship is a key subject in the Book of Revelation and there is much we can learn about how the church should worship today. There are many worship songs that use phrases from the Book of Revelation, like 'Worthy is the Lamb', 'Our God reigns' and 'Our God is a Lion, the Lion of Judah'. Sometimes we can sing these songs without understanding the full meaning behind them. Just repeating the words with a good melodic hook will not give us what we need to worship in spirit and truth. Worship should not only say 'God is good' but should also say good things about God. Between verses 1 and 6 we're given the ingredients for true worship:

1. It is God-centred.
2. It speaks of who God is.
3. It has salvation as a major theme.
4. It speaks of all aspects of God, including his judgments.
5. It declares his purpose in the earth and the nations.

6. It acknowledges the power of the throne.
7. It gives thanks for what God has done.
8. There is reverence in the presence of God.
9. It creates an environment for God to speak.
10. It is participatory (the voice of a great multitude).
11. There is an awesome sound.
12. It is multicultural (every tribe, tongue and nation).

If you read that passage with those twelve points in mind it will help you to worship!

Earlier in Revelation the references to worship and praise are building to this big event in Revelation 19. In chapters 4 and 5 we get a glimpse of the throne room in heaven, but we also connect with the church on earth. In this highly symbolic passage, we see 24 elders worshipping and singing the song in praise of the Lamb.

Ralph Martin, in his book *Worship in The Early Church*, says:

'The praise they offer in the Book of Revelation is to the holy and righteous God of Judaism who is extolled in the synagogue liturgy as creator, sustainer of the world and judge of all. The introductory phrases which the seer of Revelation uses are interesting. The verses are prefaced by such terms as: "they never ceased to sing" ... "the elders fell down on their faces and worshipped God saying", "He said with a loud voice", "They sing the song of Moses".

'All this suggests that the writer, the seer John, whom Christian tradition names as the liturgist, sought to set forth his depictions of the heavenly scene and the celestial worship by projecting onto his canvas the forms and patterns which belonged to his knowledge of the church on earth.'[30]

Ralph Martin's idea is that John's aural revelation was based on what he heard in the church. It is more likely that what John heard in his heavenly vision set the tone for what the worship of the church on earth should sound like.

THE MARRIAGE SUPPER

Revelation 18:7-10 tells us about the marriage supper of the Lamb. The relationship between God and his people has often been depicted by the imagery of a marriage. In some of the Old Testament prophetic writings Israel was sometimes described as an unfaithful wife. In the New Testament it is in the Book of Ephesians that the church is described as a bride. In Paul's teaching about marriage, he draws an analogy between the relationship of a husband and wife and Christ and the church. This verse has been quoted in chapter 4, but is relevant as we come to the marriage supper.

Ephesians 5:25-27 says:

'Husbands, love your wives, just as Christ also loved the church and gave Himself up for her, so that He might sanctify her, having cleansed her by the washing of water with the word, that He might present to Himself the church in all her glory, having no spot or wrinkle or any such thing; but that she should be holy and blameless.' (NKJV)

There is a sanctifying process going on in the church at this time as there has been through history, in order to bring the church to the place where she has made herself ready for the appearance of the bridegroom. This should motivate us to build the church carefully in true holiness. Sanctification is a process and we should have an expectation that the end-time church will be the most glorious and powerful church in history. We are sanctified through the Word, through the blood, through the work of the Holy Spirit and through our circumstances, but we also sanctify ourselves. 1 John 3:2-3 says: 'When Christ appears, we shall be like him, for we will see him just as he is. All who have this hope in him purify themselves, just as he is pure' (NIV)

Revelation 19:8 says: 'It was given to her to clothe herself in fine linen, bright and clean; for the fine linen is the righteous acts of the saints' (NASB). This is why it is so important to grow in the truth of the whole counsel of God, to be filled with the Holy Spirit, and take some responsibility ourselves. Grace is not passive. There is an active response from us.

The marriage supper of the Lamb will be a glorious feast of unimaginable delights in the presence of our heavenly bridegroom. We will be both the bride and the guest at this feast. At the moment it is as though the church is betrothed to Christ. In Bible days a betrothal was a binding agreement broken only by divorce, as in the story of Mary and Joseph. The marriage and consummation are anticipated. There is a sense in which we will not be fully the bride until this glorious consummation takes place. Meanwhile, let us be full of anticipation and ready for that glorious day.

There is an interesting cameo scene at the end of this section (Revelation 19:10) where clearly an angel has been speaking to John, yet John does not recognize him as an angel and falls at his feet to worship. However, the speaker says to him, 'Do not do that; I am a fellow servant' (NASB). This reminds us that however great the anointing on any man or woman, or any angelic visitation we may experience, it is only God who is to be worshipped. The speaker then tells John that the testimony of Jesus is the spirit of prophecy. Many have tried to give an explanation of what that means. Perhaps it could mean that prophecy is a gift that always glorifies Jesus. It never contradicts what he says and is never to be delivered in a way that contradicts his character. It could also mean that in the context of the church as the bride of Christ, the very existence of the church is a prophetic voice. The church under the anointing of the Spirit is to be a prophetic people.

JESUS RETURNS

Revelation 19:12-16 describes the coming of Jesus. This is the fulfilment of everything that has gone before.

Before we look at the details of the event as it is recorded here, we would do well to consider some of the other passages in the New Testament relating to the actual event of his coming. We will need to look at some of these in the next chapter when we come to the millennium in order to get the full picture and understand how to interpret that correctly. We understand from the gospel narrative that the expectation of the Jewish people for the coming Messiah and the new age prophesied in the Old Testament would involve a political coup, the overthrow of the Romans, and the establishing of an earthly kingdom with Israel right at the centre of world affairs. Jesus soon dispelled that notion by his actions and his teaching. The plan of God was way bigger than this, but it was not generally understood.

In the kingdom parables in Matthew's gospel, there are two parables regarding the end of the age that stand out. The first, in Matthew 13:37-40, is the parable of the wheat and the tares in which Jesus says that the kingdom of heaven is like a man who sowed good seed in his field, but when the grain grew the field also produced tares. Wheat and tares grow together. At harvest time the reapers were to gather up the tares and burn them, and then gather the wheat into the barn. In giving an explanation Jesus said,

'The one who sows the good seed is the Son of Man, and the field is the world; and as for the good seed, these are the sons of the kingdom; and the tares are the sons of the evil one; and the enemy who sowed them is the devil, and the harvest is the end of the age; and the reapers are angels. So just as the tares are gathered up and burned with fire, so shall it be at the end of the age.' (NASB)

A parable with a similar theme is the parable of the dragnet with a separation between the good fish and the bad.

Matthew 24:37-41 gives Jesus's classic teaching on the Second Coming, but a particular part of that is relevant to our view of the millennium. The Olivet discourse in Matthew 24 sees Jesus answering the question about his coming. He says:

'For the coming of the Son of Man will be just like the days of Noah. For as in those days before the flood they were eating and drinking, marrying and giving in marriage, until the day Noah entered the ark, and they did not understand until the flood came and took them all away; so will the coming of the Son of Man be. Then there will be two men in the field; one will be taken, and one will be left. Two women will be grinding at the mill; one will be taken, and one will be left.' (NASB)

The straightforward expectation and interpretation of this is that when Jesus returns it will be sudden and divisive. There will be those who are safe and those who are not. I will refer to this when we look at the different views of the millennium, but I refer to it now to establish that what we read in the Revelation vision of John about the return of Jesus, was taught by Jesus himself when he was on the earth.

Just before Jesus ascended, the disciples asked Jesus, after his resurrection, if this was now going to be the time when the kingdom would be restored to Israel. They still did not understand the bigger picture.

Jesus told them it was not for them to know the times and epochs fixed by the Father, but they were to wait for the power of the Holy Spirit to come upon them. The gospel of the kingdom was to spread to the ends of the earth before he came again.

When he ascended two angels told the disciples that Jesus would return in just the same way he had ascended.

The epistles make frequent reference to the coming of the Lord, and the Early Church was looking for his imminent return. There are three Greek words used in connection with the Second Coming, and each gives a slightly different perspective to the same event. Revelation draws from the meaning of all these words together in this cataclysmic finale to the end of the age as we know it.

The most common word is 'parousia'. This is a word describing the arrival of a king, an emperor, a great ruler. In Kittel's *Theological Dictionary of the New Testament* he says: 'On the occasion of such visits, there are flattering speeches, delicacies to eat, asses for the baggage, street improvements, wreaths and gifts of money. Under the empire the ceremonies become even more magnificent and visits are marked by new buildings, and the institution of holy days. That word seems to be the nearest word on a human level to describe what will be an indescribable event. *Parousia* comes the closest.'[31]

This is the word Paul uses in 1 Thessalonians 4:13-17.

'We do not want you to be uninformed, brethren, about those who are asleep, so that you will not grieve as do the rest who have no hope. For if we believe that Jesus died and rose again, even so God will bring with Him those who have fallen asleep in Jesus. For this we say to you by the word of the Lord, that we who are alive and remain until the coming (*parousia*) of the Lord, will not precede those who have fallen asleep. For the Lord Himself will descend from heaven with a shout, with the

The Unveiling

voice of the archangel and with the trumpet of God, and the dead in Christ will rise first. Then we who are alive and remain will be caught up together with them in the clouds to meet the Lord in the air, and so we shall always be with the Lord.' (NASB)

In 1 Corinthians 15:20-23 Paul says that believers will be resurrected at the 'parousia'.

Another word connected with the Second Coming is 'epiphaneia'. This means to show oneself. It denotes a public appearance, a visible reality. There will be nothing secretive about Jesus's return. This word is used several times in connection with the coming of Jesus and in 2 Thessalonians 2:8 it is used in connection with his slaying of the lawless one, the Antichrist, with his breath. (Whether we believe there is an actual person who is the Antichrist or whether this is a reference to the spirit of Antichrist operating through the people and systems of this world, the victory will be complete.)

It says: 'Then that lawless one will be revealed whom the Lord will slay with the breath of His mouth and bring to an end by the appearance [epiphaneia] of His coming' (NASB).

The third word used is 'apokalupsis' which means to reveal. It is a full disclosure. Robert Letham suggests that the use of 'apokalupsis' brings a greater focus on judgment.[32]

2 Thessalonians 1:7-8 says that God will 'give relief to you who are afflicted and to us as well when the Lord Jesus will be revealed [apokalupsis] from heaven with His mighty angels in flaming fire, dealing out retribution to those who do not know God and to those who do not obey the gospel' (NASB).

There are other passages, notably 2 Peter chapter 3, which give us accounts of the Second Coming and the end of the age.

In Revelation we get all of these thoughts combining as Jesus arrives with the name King of Kings and Lord of Lords in Revelation 19:16. He is the one who is faithful and true, who has conquered and

126

overthrown Satan and his demonic hordes. He is the one whose eyes are as flaming fire penetrating into the depths of every human heart. On his head are the diadems and crowns of eternal kingship. His robe dipped in blood speaks of his own suffering for our sin, but also the blood of his enemies as he brings about this awesome judgment. Out of his mouth comes the sharp two-edged sword and as he speaks, he strikes down nations and governments who have opposed him.

In verse 12 we are told he has a name that no one knows, except himself. Possibly a reference to the mystery of the relationship between the Father and the Son. In Luke 10 after the return of the mission outreach of the seventy-two disciples (Luke 10:17-20) we see Jesus rejoicing in the Holy Spirit, and as he communes with his Father, we catch a glimpse of this glorious mystery.

'I thank you, Father, Lord of heaven and earth, that you have hidden these things from the wise and understanding and revealed them to little children; yes, Father, for such was your gracious will. All things have been handed over to me by my Father, and no one knows the Son except the Father, and no one knows the Father except the Son and anyone to whom the Son chooses to reveal him.' (Matthew 11:25 ESV)

In the coming of Christ in Revelation 19, this mystery is revealed in two titles.

The first is that he is named 'The Word of God'. This title is used of Jesus at the beginning of John's gospel.

'In the beginning was the Word, and the Word was with God, and the Word was God. He was in the beginning with God. All things came into being through Him, and apart from Him nothing came into being that has come into being.' (John1:1-3 NASB)

The Son of God, the second person in the Trinity, has always been the Word of God from all eternity. Genesis shows us that the world was made through him and in Proverbs 8:27-30 we see the personification of the Word as an agent of creation, at one with the Father.

> 'When He established the heavens, I was there,
> When He inscribed a circle in the face of the deep,
> When He made firm the skies above,
> When the springs of the deep became fixed,
> When He set for the sea its boundary
> So that the water would not transgress His command,
> When He marked out the foundations of the earth;
> Then I was beside Him, as a master workman;
> And I was daily His delight,
> Rejoicing always before Him.' (NASB)

Jesus the Word was not only active in creation, he was the living Word active throughout the whole of the Old Testament.

In John's gospel 1:14 we read, 'The Word became flesh, and dwelt among us, and we saw His glory, glory as of the only begotten from the Father, full of grace and truth' (NASB).

The Word becoming flesh meant that the eternal Son of God was now taking on the frailty of human flesh. When he emptied himself into our world in the incarnation, he did not empty himself of divinity, as some have suggested. He remained fully God while becoming fully man. He took upon himself servanthood and ministered with a voluntary dependency on the Holy Spirit. His choice to live as a human meant that like all of us he felt pain, he wept, he got tired and hungry. He ministered as a man filled with the Holy Spirit, choosing to live within human limitations, and it was the Spirit's power that enabled him to work miracles. This should encourage us to believe that under the anointing of the Spirit we can continue to do the works that Jesus did, as he promised. No one can ever duplicate the ministry of Jesus, but we can expect God to use us in the supernatural because Jesus has gone before us and released the power of the Spirit at Pentecost.

But some miracles were exceptional. There were times when Jesus's divinity shone through, but only to those who had eyes to see. The miracle of turning water into wine shows the truth of who Jesus is dawning in the hearts and minds of the disciples. John 2:11 says, 'This beginning of His signs Jesus did in Cana of Galilee, and manifested His glory, and His disciples believed in Him' (NASB) showing Jesus to be the promised Messianic new wine.

William Hendrickson in his commentary on this verse says: 'It indicates a miracle viewed as a proof of divine authority and majesty.'[33]

John's gospel is built around a series of miracles called 'signs'. The signs point to who Jesus is. The loaves and fishes show us that Jesus is the bread of life and the new manna. The healing of the blind man shows him to be the light of the world, and the raising of Lazarus shows he is the resurrection and the Life.

Our understanding in Revelation 19 of Jesus having a name 'The Word of God' should embrace his eternal sonship, his activity in the Old Testament that he is God's articulated speech to the human race in his humanity, but now in his Second Coming he is the Word spoken to the whole human race. Not only to those who love him but to all who have disowned him.

Jesus is and was the eternal Word made flesh, glorified through his death, resurrection and ascension, now reigning in heaven as our glorious prophet, priest and king, awaiting that moment when he will burst through the heavens, with the revelation of the second name that is given to him: KING OF KINGS AND LORD OF LORDS.

It was this passage of Scripture in Revelation 19 that inspired my song 'In Majesty He Comes'.

In majesty he comes, the Lamb who once was slain.
Riding in victory, faithful and true,
Eyes ablaze, crowns on his head.
Robe dipped in blood from his suffering
He is the Word of God
Coming again
King of Kings.
We shall rise, we shall meet him in the air
When he comes again.
And we will worship him, worship him
Give him praise forevermore.
King of Kings and Lord of Lords.
(Copyright © 1990 Thankyou Music)[34]

I was invited to do a week's teaching in Singapore, by Jimmy and Carol Owens the writers of *Come Together* and *If My people*, two musical productions that had a massive impact on the church in the late Seventies and early Eighties.

The week was to end with a concert where I would lead worship and speak. I was working with a very talented American band who had been invited to accompany me. I had taken a drummer from my worship band in Brighton who added some extra percussion to the band from America. The event was going well but the audience although attentive were passive. I was longing for God to break into what was a formal concert. After teaching this song, which the audience picked up reasonably quickly, I began to read Revelation 19 over the auditorium. As I was reading, my drummer from Brighton began to improvise a drum solo behind the reading. In a moment the atmosphere changed, and the drama of the reading was captured by the prophetic drumming. It was rather like the episode in Elisha's ministry in 2 Kings 3 when the prophet called for a minstrel, and as he played, the hand of the Lord came upon the prophet.

As the drummer played and the reading was proclaimed, people began to rush forward for prayer in that packed auditorium. That night many were saved, many were filled with the Holy Spirit and there were several healings.

The power of the Scripture being read, accompanied by the prophetic musicians, created a platform for the Holy Spirit to move and many encountered God in a new way. It seemed to anticipate that great day when Jesus returns to the whole world, named as the KING OF KINGS AND LORD OF LORDS.

CHAPTER 14
WHAT ABOUT THE MILLENNIUM?
Read Revelation 19:17-21 and 20:1-6

Chapter 19 ends with a graphic description of all the enemies of Christ and his church being overthrown, utterly defeated. The beast, the false prophet and everything associated with them are thrown into the lake of fire.

We now come to chapter 20 which is probably the most controversial chapter in the whole book. There are those who regard chapter 20 as following on chronologically from chapter 19 indicating that after Jesus has returned, the 'millennial kingdom' on the earth will be established for 1,000 years, during which Satan will remain bound. After the 1,000 years are finished Satan will be let loose, there will be a huge war and then the judgment at the great white throne will occur.

However, there are others who would say, following the pattern of a 'non-chronological approach', that Revelation 20:1-6 is a parenthesis between the end of Revelation 19 and Revelation 20:7 where we read about the millennium. There are four main ways of interpreting these six verses and arguments supporting these views. This enables us to suggest what is the most logical, as well as theological interpretation and why.

CLASSIC PRE-MILLENIALISM

Pre-millennialists fall into two categories (and just to really complicate things even within those categories, there are sub-categories).

Classic pre-millennialists, simply put, believe that before Jesus returns, the world will be evangelized, Israel will be converted, there will be a time of great persecution and the Antichrist will appear.

The *Parousia* will then happen, the dead saints will be resurrected, the Antichrist will be overthrown, Israel will be restored to its own land and be prominent. Jesus will then reign on earth literally and physically for a thousand years. Sin will be limited. The lion will lie with the lamb. This will be a time of incredible blessing for the world.

At the end of this time Satan will be loosed, the wicked resurrected and the final judgment will then take place.

DISPENSATIONAL PRE-MILLENIALISM

This theory emerged in the nineteenth century from an Irish Anglican, J.N. Darby, who became the leader of the Plymouth Brethren. He developed a system of reading the Bible from the perspective of different dispensations or time periods. The Scofield Reference Bible was produced, based on Darby's ideas.

His teachings are too complicated to develop here so I will cover them from the perspective of the millennium as succinctly as I can. Dispensational Pre-millennialists would say that the Book of Revelation is not to be interpreted as an unfolding of the panorama of history but is directed towards the events just prior to Jesus's return. There is a very strong emphasis on the nation of Israel and the return of the Jews to their own land. The Last Days will be marked by a seven-year period of what they call the 'Great Tribulation' where the beast, the Antichrist and the false prophet will be prominent. At this point the system becomes complicated because some believe that the church will be what they call 'raptured' before the tribulation starts and escape it. There are others who believe that the church will be 'raptured' after three and a half years of the tribulation. So, there is a first stage to Jesus's coming whether pre-tribulation or post-tribulation. At the end of the tribulation Satan will be bound for 1,000 years and Jesus will reign on the earth in Jerusalem, the Jewish Temple will be restored, and sacrifices will be made once again. However, the sacrifices will be considered as a memorial and not redemptive, because the Jews will now believe in the redemptive work of Christ. At the end of the thousand years Satan will be loosed and the judgment will take place before the great white throne.

Many evangelicals have been taught this theory and American evangelicalism is still rife with this teaching today. Anyone with a Brethren background will have been taught this and the Scofield Reference Bible is full of notes from this perspective.

The positive side to this is that at least the redemptive work of Christ in salvation is strongly upheld. However, from both the logical and theological perspective, it makes no sense. Firstly, Israel being given such prominence is a denial of the New Covenant and the rebuilding of the Temple and resurgence of animal sacrifices is a total denial of the teaching of Jesus and of the epistles. It would seem that Jesus comes again at least twice in this system of thought and the idea of a rapture with people being taken out of the earth while others are left is just not in the Bible. There is no biblical evidence for a rapture and the word does not even appear in Scripture. Every single reference from the gospels through the epistles and into Revelation all see the one event.

Those who believe in a rapture will quote Matthew 24 where it says, 'Then there will be two men in the field; one will be taken and one will be left. Two women will be grinding at the mill; one will be taken and one will be left' (Matthew 24:40-41 NASB).

In the previous verse Jesus uses the example of Noah, and when the flood came it was a cataclysmic disaster. The division was clear. People were either in the ark and safe or left outside. The illustration does not show that when Jesus returns some will be left on the earth. Just as when the floods came in the time of Noah it was too late, so when Jesus returns, if people are not ready it will be too late.

Jesus returns, the dead are resurrected, Satan is overthrown, the judgment takes place and the wicked are sent to hell and the new heaven and the new earth become the dwelling place of the redeemed. Classic pre-millennialists have a stronger argument than dispensational pre-millennialists, but both arguments are weak, as we shall see.

POST MILLENIALISM

Post-millennialists believe that Jesus will return after the millennium. They have an expectation of a golden age where the world will have been evangelized and that there will be a 'Christianizing' of the whole world. When Jesus eventually returns it will be to a world that is ready to receive him.

There is an attractiveness about post-millennialism because it makes us optimistic about the spread of the gospel. Post-millennialists believe in a massive end-time revival that affects all areas of society, the arts, the media, and the governments of the world. There will be peace on earth for a lengthy period of time. There are several so-called popular prophetic movements today that teach and preach from this perspective. Unfortunately, optimism is not necessarily biblical, and we have to hold in tension the fact that we need to pray for revival and for the gospel to reach the nations, but this is in the context of tribulation, opposition and persecution of the church and the gospel. We are to be neither pessimists nor optimists, but men and women of faith who take our expectations from what the Bible teaches.

AMILLINENNIALISM

Amillennialists believe, as others who have interpreted Revelation, that the period of one thousand years is not to be taken literally and that Revelation 20:1-6 is symbolic of the period between the Ascension and the Second Coming. It should actually encourage us to believe for a manifestation and demonstration of the kingdom of God in the whole earth, before Jesus returns. When Jesus told us to pray: 'Your kingdom come, your will be done on earth as it is in heaven', this is an eschatological prayer for the new heaven and the new earth but with a manifestation of that in the present. It is an 'already and not yet' prayer.

The binding of Satan here is a reference to his defeat at the cross. As Jesus was foretelling his death, he says in John 12:31, 'Now judgment is upon this world; now the ruler of this world will be cast down' (NASB).

In Mark 3:26-27 when Jesus had been casting out demons he said, 'If Satan has risen up against himself and is divided, he cannot stand, but he is finished! But no one can enter the strong man's house and plunder his property unless he first binds the strong man, and then he will plunder his house' (NASB). Jesus bound the strong man at the cross. The word 'bind' here is the same word that is used at the beginning of Revelation 20. We do not bind Satan. Jesus has already done it at the cross. The passage about the millennium is picture language for the church age. Satan is a defeated foe. We stand in Christ's victory. Yes, Satan does have a sphere. The chain has a length, but it can only go so far. Revelation 20 should encourage us to look forward to the great day of Jesus's return and realize that as a kingdom of priests we stand in Christ's victory and even when we go through tribulation, and even martyrdom, if we hold fast to him and his word we shall reign with Christ.

For the sake of unity with our brothers and sisters, it is important for us to be open-hearted towards those who have a different millennial view from us as long as they are not denying basic evangelical belief. But it is important for us to know what we believe, so the essentials are:

1. Jesus will return.
2. Satan and all wickedness will be overthrown.
3. The church is to stand in the victory of Christ.
4. Tribulations and trials will come.
5. God will pour out his ongoing judgments.
6. The gospel of the kingdom will be preached to all nations.
7. We should live with the expectation of his return and live our lives accordingly.

I conclude this chapter by quoting from Revelation 19:11-16 so that we lift our eyes to the glorious triumph of our king.

'And I saw heaven opened, and behold, a white horse, and He who sat on it is called Faithful and True, and in righteousness He judges and wages war. His eyes are a flame of fire, and on His head are many diadems; and He has a name written on Him which no one knows except Himself. He is clothed with a robe dipped in blood, and His name is called The Word of God. And the armies which are in heaven, clothed in fine linen, white and clean, were following Him on white horses. From His mouth comes a sharp sword, so that with it He may strike down the nations, and He will rule them with a rod of iron; and He treads the wine press of the fierce wrath of God, the Almighty. And on His robe and on His thigh he has a name written, "KING OF KINGS, AND LORD OF LORDS."' (NASB)

CHAPTER 15
RESURGAM
Read Revelation 21 and 22

One of the joys of living in Brighton for over fifty years was breathing the sea air. When I was a young student living in Kemp Town, just a stone's throw from the eastern end of the seafront, I would frequently go down to the beach early in the morning to watch the sunrise and also to pray. I often found that if I needed some particular guidance or had issues that I was seeking to work through, Brighton beach early in the morning was my sanctuary. With the waves breaking, and the sucking and flinging of the pebbles, this was a place where spiritual battles would be fought and won. I used to recall that it was on Brighton beach that Hudson Taylor heard God calling him to go to China. Some mornings when the wind was howling and the sea was particularly rough, the sense of power in the surging waves gave me an overwhelming sense of the majesty and grandeur of a mighty God.

One morning I was there and to my horror the sea had washed up a dead body. There it was, a lifeless corpse, naked, tossed around in the waves like a discarded piece of flotsam. Someone spotted it before I did, and a policeman was soon on the scene. He waded into the water and grabbed the leg of the dead person and dragged it up the pebbles as though it were a sack of potatoes or any lump of rubbish. What shocked me was the absolute lifelessness of the corpse. Someone who had been a living, breathing, feeling, human being. They must have had a father, a mother, perhaps a family and friends but now here was a lifeless lump of what the great Professor Joad once called, in his description of the human body, 'Enough water to fill a ten-gallon barrel, enough fat for seven bars of soap, carbon for

9,000 lead pencils, phosphorous for 2,200 match heads, iron for a medium-sized nail, lime enough to whitewash a hen coop and a little of magnesium and sulphur.'

As the scene unfolded before me, I was reminded of the poem by Ted Hughes, the one-time Poet Laureate, 'View of a Pig'. The poem begins: *'The pig lay on a barrow, dead.'* One of the stanzas says:

'It was too dead. Just so much
A poundage of lard and pork.
Its last dignity had entirely gone
It was not a figure of fun.'[35]

I had studied this poem for A-level English Literature, and here, in this tragic morning scene, the symbolism of death, its total finality, gripped me.

There seemed no difference between the dead pig and this lump of flesh dragged out of the waves. 'It was too dead.'

A lifeless corpse speaks of finality, the end. No more speaking, enjoyment of a good meal, thinking, appreciation of music or a sunset, family celebrations, laughter or tears. All finished.

Sadly, the human race is dominated by the nihilistic pessimism of Ted Hughes. The Bible tells a different story, and it is in the Book of Revelation that all the teaching of Scripture comes together in the glorious consummation of the ages, with the promise of eternal life in the new heavens and new earth.

As we have journeyed through the Book of Revelation, we have seen that it is not just about the end of the end times and the Second Coming of Jesus. It is a book that unfolds the panorama of history as it tells the story of the world in all its corrupt sinfulness. It's the story of the church and its victory. It tells of the fact that God has a plan and purpose worked out through Jesus the Lamb slain for our sin, the conquering Lion who rules over everything. God is drawing history to a divine conclusion, the summing up of everything under the headship of Christ. Every human being who has ever lived will one day stand before God and there will be a day of accountability.

The Bible shows us clearly that physical death is not the end. Although there are many who believe that death is the end in the way the Ted Hughes poem suggests. There is also an instinctive feeling in many that there could be some sort of life after death. There are belief systems from other religions, the occult, and even human optimism that give us such concepts as reincarnation and the immortality of the soul.

One of the most popular songs at the funerals of people who are not Christians is Robbie Williams' 'Angels'. He wrote this song with Guy Chambers, although later, after the song's success, there were some arguments about who had actually written it. It is probably Robbie Williams' biggest song, and the words offer an optimistic hope and comfort to the bereaved, which is why it is so popular at funerals. Unfortunately, the words have no biblical credibility and offer only false hope and comfort. In his own words Robbie Williams said: 'I believed that stuff when I wrote "Angels" – that's why I wrote it. "Angels" isn't about anybody, it's about the thoughts that loved ones that have passed on come back and take care of you.'

Also popular at funerals is the poem by Henry Scott Holland, 'Death is Nothing at All'.

> 'Death is nothing at all
> It does not count
> I have only slipped away to the next room . . .
> I am I, and you are you . . .
> Whatever we were to each other
> That we still are.' [36]

Sadly, this again only brings false comfort. The concept of the immortality of the soul is not a biblical expression or concept. Biblical immortality is based on resurrection. Ultimately, when we die, our eternal life will be lived out in our new resurrected bodies and we will look at this in more detail in a later chapter.

This then raises the question: what happens to us when we die? There are three main views.

1. Annihilation (we have touched on this already).
2. We go to sleep (the word 'cemetery' is a Greek word meaning 'sleeping place').
3. There is a place where if we are born-again Christians, our soul/spirit continues to exist in the presence of God, enjoying the delights of heaven, but waiting in eager anticipation for our eternal destiny. Those who are not Christians will be in a place separated from God awaiting the day of judgment.

The one thing we can be clear about is that when we die and exit this world, we do enter another. For the Christian, it is an entrance into the presence of God. In Luke 23:43, Jesus told the dying thief: 'Today you will be with me in paradise' (NIV).

When a person dies without Christ, they enter a place of separation from God, but both non-Christians and Christians are in one place or another waiting for the day when Jesus returns and all the dead everywhere will be raised. The resurrection of the dead leads to everyone being judged.

Revelation 20:11-15 says:

'Then I saw a great white throne and Him who sat on it, from whose presence earth and heaven fled away, and no place was found for them. And I saw the dead, the great and the small, standing before the throne, and books were opened; and another book was opened, which is the book of life; and the dead were judged from the things which were written in the books, according to their deeds. And the sea gave up the dead which were in it, and death and Hades gave up the dead which were in them; and they were judged, every one of them according to their deeds. Then death and Hades were thrown into the lake of fire. This is the second death, the lake of fire. And if anyone's name was not found written in the book of life, he was thrown into the lake of fire.' (NASB)

We can conclude from this passage that the resurrection and the final judgment are connected events which are also referred to in several other passages of Scripture.

The resurrection of Jesus is of course essential for the Christian faith, and in 1 Corinthians 15 Paul says that the death, burial and resurrection of Jesus are of first importance. When we are born again, we are risen with Christ. His life is in us, but it is not just that we have the 'now' experience of Christ in us. When he returns, we shall be raised from the dead and we will have a body that will be like the risen Lord Jesus. The gospel narrative shows how he was totally recognizable. The two friends on the Emmaus road were walking and talking with a human being, not a ghost or a spirit. When Jesus met the disciples on the seashore, he was cooking breakfast and eating fish.

When we are resurrected our bodies will no longer be subject to decay; we shall be raised incorruptible, we shall be glorified, radiant, dazzling even. We cannot possibly imagine what that will look like or feel like, but it will be glorious. We will no longer become weary, weak or sick, and yet we will have a physical body.

Hoekema says in his book *The Bible and the Future*:

'If the resurrection body were non-material or non-physical, the devil would have won a great victory since God would have been compelled to change human beings with physical bodies such as he had created into creatures of a different sort, without physical bodies (like the angels). Then it would seem that matter had become intrinsically evil so that it had to be banished. And then, in a sense, the Greek philosophers would have been proved right. But matter is not evil; it is part of God's good creation. Therefore, the goal of God's good creation is the resurrection of the physical body, and the creation of a new earth on which his redeemed people can live and serve God forever with glorified bodies.'[37]

In 1 Corinthians 15, Paul speaks about the resurrection body and he draws a contrast between the natural and the spiritual. His concern here is not about the resurrection of unbelievers but believers and the kind of bodies that they will have. He says about the resurrected body:

'It is sown a perishable body, it is raised an imperishable body; it is sown in dishonour, it is raised in glory; it is sown in weakness, it is raised in power; it is sown a natural body, it is raised a spiritual body. If there is a natural body, there is also a spiritual body. So also it is written, "The first MAN Adam BECAME A LIVING SOUL." The last Adam, a life-giving spirit.' (1 Corinthians 15:42-45 NASB)

Here we have the contrast between a natural body ('*soma psychikon*') and a spiritual body ('*soma pneumatikos*'). Here the word 'spiritual' does not mean non-physical but rather someone who is guided by and filled with the Holy Spirit. What Paul seems to be saying here is that our resurrected body will be '*psychicos*', natural, but also '*pneumatikos*', spiritual. Quoting Hoekema again, he observes that 'the spiritual body of the resurrection will be one which will be totally, not just partially dominated and directed by the Holy Spirit'.[38] There will be a different level of existence for us and we cannot speculate as to exactly what our resurrected bodies will be like. What we do know is that there will be both continuity and identity.

1 Corinthians 15:20 says that 'Christ has been raised from the dead, the first fruits of those who are asleep' (NASB). The first fruits of a harvest anticipate the greater harvest to come and are exactly the same as what is to come. The resurrection of Jesus guarantees ours. When we were 'in Adam', the end result would have been death, but because we are now 'in Christ' the end result is resurrection.

I have already said that resurrection and judgment are to be seen as two parts of one event, and we do not know exactly the details of how that works. What we can be sure of is that all will be raised, and all will be judged.

The concepts of judgment, reward and punishment are seen clearly in the Bible but in recent years there have been many objections and discussions regarding the outworking of this, even amongst evangelical theologians.

The simple concept of the saved, born-again, Bible-believing Christian going to heaven while the unsaved go to hell has raised all sorts of questions about the love of God and his justice. What is clear from the Book of Revelation and many other Scriptures is that all will be judged and there will be rewards and exclusions or punishments. Christians will be judged according to their works, but this does not mean judgment of each action in isolation. It would seem from 2 Corinthians 5:10 that 'we must all appear before the judgment seat of Christ, so that each one may be recompensed for his deeds in the body, according to what he has done, whether good or bad' (NASB). Robert Letham suggests that the grammar of this sentence indicates it is a holistic judgment relating to the whole of life rather than individual actions in isolation.[39]

As Christians we are not to be afraid of judgment, because our sins have been dealt with. We will not have our sins called out, paraded before the whole of creation for all to see. When we appear before the judgment seat of Christ we will have been glorified already. In fact, we will be called upon to participate in the judgment of angels. The mind cannot comprehend what this will look like. It is clear that God as judge will bring his verdict over our lives, and those who are saved, whatever accusations the devil may have made, will be totally safe. However, there will be rewards and our works will have been tried in the fire. The gold and silver will remain. The wood, hay and stubble will be burned. The concept of judgment should motivate us, not out of terror or shame, but out of an assurance that God is always loving, righteous and just.

There can be no doubt that those who are not Christians will be separated and will receive their future destiny based on God's wisdom and justice. The traditional Augustinian view for the unsaved, that 'one size fits all' when it comes to eternal punishment, is questionable. What we do know is that it is the redeemed, glorified citizens of the new creation who will inhabit the eternal city. It could be argued when it comes to unbelievers, that there will be those who are left outside the city and those who will burn in the lake of fire. We would do well not to speculate, but to remember that God is always just. What is not either speculative or negotiable is that the redeemed will inhabit the new heavens and the new earth, and the unredeemed will be in a separate place.

After the resurrection of the dead and the final judgment we come to the final two chapters of Revelation. Revelation 20 begins with the new heaven and earth and then gives us a description of the new Jerusalem. In chapter 21 we gain a glimpse of the quality of life we will enjoy in eternity and the Revelation vision ends with an exhortation, a challenge and a warning.

CHAPTER 16
THE NEW HEAVEN AND EARTH
Read Revelation 21:1-9

We could say that the Bible ends where it began. The first two chapters of Genesis, with their description of creation and the Garden of Eden, show us a heaven and earth that mankind was intended to inhabit, cultivate and care for. The plan of God was that Adam and Eve should be fruitful and multiply and their mandate was to extend Eden. God had so created the earth that all the resources of creation would be at Adam's disposal to fulfil the mandate that God had given. The earth was also to be the Temple, the place where the eternal, glorious maker of heaven and earth, who had made man in his own image, and breathed his own breath into him to give him life, would dwell with the being he had created. Earth was to be the dwelling place of God. It was to be a dwelling place that spoke of relationship, because God is omnipresent. His dwelling on earth with Adam was relational. This elevated this feature of God's creativity, beyond all other aspects and dimensions of his creative powers. Adam was to rule over what God had made, he was to be the mouthpiece of praise for the rest of creation, and his power of speech was to give vocal expression to the plans and purposes of God. Adam enjoyed a loving relationship with God as they walked together in the cool of the day. This made Adam a king, a priest, a prophet. As king he was delegated to rule, as priest he articulated praise, as prophet he could hear God speak and declare what he was saying. The relationship with Eve, his wife, was to be a union of one flesh, man and woman together complementing each other to see God's plan and purpose to be fruitful and multiply being fulfilled.

When the fall happened and sin came in, this was a devastating and catastrophic event that not only separated Adam and Eve from God but put the whole of creation out of joint. From Genesis 3 to Revelation 21, we have the effects of the catastrophe played out in the history of the human race.

It is in the Old Testament that we learn of God's plan progressively revealed to remedy this calamitous event. The promise of a second Adam, a redeemer, would be revealed through the Law and the prophets, contained within the covenant promises made to Abraham and worked out in the forming of a people who would fulfil his original purpose. However, as the Bible story unfolds, we see one spiritual disaster after another.

In spite of the human catastrophe of the sinfulness of the human race, God's promises are being fulfilled. The redeemer has come, God has a people who love him. The nations receive the gospel.

The plan of salvation, the coming of Jesus, the cross, resurrection and ascension, the outpouring of the Holy Spirit and the formation of the church were all part of the process to bring creation back to its original order and purpose. Revelation 20 and 21 sees Eden restored, the curse finally and completely nullified and a multitude from every tribe, tongue and nation living in a regenerated new heaven and earth.

There are many prophetic passages in the Old Testament that speak of all this. Perhaps the clearest passage is Isaiah 65:17-18 where, following the promise of the Messiah and all that he would suffer to bring salvation, we have this great promise:

'Behold, I create new heavens and a new earth; and the former things will not be remembered or come to mind. But be glad and rejoice in what I create; for behold, I create Jerusalem for rejoicing and her people for gladness.' (NASB)

As the old world passes away, Revelation 21:1 tells us there will be no more sea. For John the sea would speak of separation. The sea has been a place where nations have traded, a place of the dead and a place of judgment. The Red Sea and its destruction of the armies of Pharaoh is often used symbolically. G.K. Beale suggests that the sea is figurative of 'old world' threats, adding: 'This means that the presence of a literal sea in the new creation would not be inconsistent with the figurative "no sea".'[40]

The prophecy then goes on to describe Jerusalem and the quality of life to be enjoyed in this new heaven and earth and the city within it. No more weeping, no more tensions in the natural world, trade and family life will continue. All the realities of life without the pains and situations that would ruin it. This prophecy parallels Revelation 21.

A question that many theologians have wrestled with is whether the new heavens and the new earth will be completely new, with the old totally destroyed. There have been many arguments put forward for both sides of the case, but the stronger is for a renewal of the earth, not a destruction.

When God made the earth in the first place, he called it good. In commenting on the passage in 1 Peter 1:7-8, Peter says that the idea of fire there is to purify. Those who argue that the cosmos will be destroyed by the fire of God's judgment, have not noted that fire purifies as well as destroys. Robert Letham says: 'Whatever the eventual reality, the argument for a literal destruction of the cosmos and its replacement by a new one cannot be sustained from a reading of this passage or any other. Rather the "all things" that will be headed up by Christ (Ephesians 1:10) will consist of the very things he created.'[41]

When Jesus was discussing some issues concerning the future and eternity with the disciples (Matthew 19:28) he said: 'Truly I say to you, that you who have followed Me, in the regeneration [NIV 'renewal'] when the Son of Man will sit on His glorious throne, you also shall sit upon twelve thrones, judging the twelve tribes of Israel' (NASB). The word translated 'regeneration', or in some versions, 'renewal', is 'palingenesia'. This is a joining of two words 'palin' and 'genesis', meaning a return to existence or renewal to a higher existence.[42]

The new heavens and new earth will be a second Genesis. There are many other passages of Scripture that express the same idea.

The renewal of the present Cosmos shows us the complete and utter defeat of Satan. If the heavens and earth had been totally destroyed, Satan would have won a great victory. There is no such victory. God will renew, restore and regenerate what he started.

Chapter 21:2 sees the holy city, the new Jerusalem, coming down out of heaven from God. The holy city is described as a 'bride made ready', adorned for her husband (NASB).

Both the new heavens and earth and the new Jerusalem fulfil the idea we looked at in Genesis 1 and 2 that God was making his abode, his dwelling place, here on earth.

Revelation 21:22 says: 'I saw no temple in it, for the Lord God the Almighty and the Lamb are its temple' (NASB).

The description of the holy city is full of imagery. The precious stones speak of a bride adorned with the stones that were in the original Temple.

These stones suggest God's redeeming work where he beautifies his bride, in contrast to the fallen harlot Babylon.

The dimensions of the city show it to be a cube, and this is symbolic of eternal security and indestructability.

The overarching theme here is the glorious presence of God. There is so much detail in this chapter and further study will help to clarify more of the symbolism. The important things to remember are that we who are redeemed will be there as the bride, adorned and made beautiful. There will be a separation and exclusion of those who have rejected Christ.

We will be in a conscious place with all the beauties of creation without any hint of sin or suffering. We will know and recognize each other, and all the joys of earth we have now will be ours. Central to our experience will be our enjoyment in every moment of the realized presence of God. The Lamb will be a constant reminder of how we have entered into this glorious bliss of the purified. Life in the new heavens and new earth will have everything wonderful about life on the earth as we know it. There will be no tears, no sickness, no death. There will be a river of life running through causing abundant fruitfulness and trees with leaves that will heal tensions between nations and races. All nations will live together in harmony with God and each other. How can the human mind take this in? All we can do is bring our worship and praise to the One who will surely fulfil all this. He will end the story, so that the real story can begin.

The vision ends with an exhortation and challenge. The Book of Revelation has been neglected but the last section begins with the words: 'Do not seal up the words of the prophecy of this book for the time is near' (Revelation 22:10 NASB). There is a diagnosis of the world which suggests that many will not change in Revelation 22:11: 'Let the one who does wrong, still do wrong; and let the one who is filthy, still be filthy; and let the one who is righteous still practice righteousness; and the one who is holy, still keep himself holy'(NASB).

The world will continue with the polarization of light and darkness, righteousness and unrighteousness, the church and the world, Babylon and Jerusalem. The contrasts could go on and on. Revelation 22:14-15 sums up all of this:

'Blessed are those who wash their robes, so that they may have the right to the tree of life, and may enter by the gates into the city. Outside are the dogs and the sorcerers [Greek 'pharmakos' –

drug dealers and occult practitioners] and the immoral persons and the murderers and the idolaters, and everyone who loves and practices lying.' (NASB)

If we made a comprehensive word study on all of these categories, we would find the whole human race without Christ.

We are exhorted to take this vision seriously and we must not add or take away from all the theological concepts implied in this book, and there are dire warnings to anyone who does.

CHAPTER 17
EVERY TRIBE AND EVERY TONGUE

It is worship that enhances our joys, sustains us in our sorrows, gives hope in our uncertainties, victories in our battles, befriends us in our loneliness, reassures us in our need to be loved, captivates us in our encounters with God, releases us when we need to repent, envisions us when we look to the future, builds faith when we sing his word. God made us to be worshippers because he made us for relationship.

Worship is a major theme in the Book of Revelation, and with all the mystery of the visions, symbols, seals, trumpets, bowls, beasts and dragons we must make sure that we do not miss the central theme that we are to be worshippers. Our love and devotion are to a wonderful Father who unfolds his plan for the whole world, of the glorious Son who shed his blood in sacrificial lamb-like humility, and yet roars lion-like in his victory over the powers of darkness.

We worship in the power of the Spirit who floods us and fills us and gives us the foretaste of our future glory.

The multitude described as singing the song of the Lamb should inspire us to be, in the words of Stuart Townend's wonderful song 'Beautiful Saviour', 'longing to be where the praise is never-ending' (copyright © 1998 Thankyou Music).[43]

A particularly poignant time of singing this was at the thanksgiving service of a very dear friend. Her name was Lorrie and I had known her since she was a teenager. She was in our church youth group when I was an elder in the church in Brighton. Even as a teenager she had an amazing voice, and after training to be a music teacher she sang as a soprano soloist in many of my musical productions including Handel's *Messiah*. Lorrie was a real worshipper and during the weeks leading up to her death she had a very close walk with God. The last time I saw her alive she quoted Stuart's song with a profound serenity and expectancy.

We had prayed many times for her healing and although I have seen cancers healed along with many other miracles, for Lorrie the Father had another purpose. The day she went to be with Jesus I was on holiday in Spain, and that night I had a vision. Lorrie has four daughters who all sing beautifully. In the vision I saw Lorrie on her bed, with her husband Steve and four daughters standing around her. They were all singing and worshipping and suddenly four angels appeared and joined in the song. They then gently lifted her and carried her into heaven still singing. She was carried into a bright light and then I was not allowed to see beyond that veil. She truly went to the place where the praise is never-ending and joined with the countless worshippers singing the songs she loved on earth, but now in the reality of the presence of the Lord she loved.

The Book of Revelation gives us glimpses into our destiny and our worship here on earth anticipates what we will enjoy in eternity. Not that we will spend eternity singing worship songs as we see in the chapter on the new heavens and new earth, but I am sure there will be times when the whole company of the redeemed will gather in a great symphony of praise.

In anticipation of those glorious days ahead, the church on earth is to be flooded with worship.

I have been involved in worship ministry for nearly seventy years, starting as a very little boy playing cornet in the Salvation Army band. Singing and playing an instrument to give expression to my love for God was passed on to me by my parents and my father's parents who were church planters in the revival in the late 1800s and early 1900s when the Salvation Army saw over four thousand churches planted in just a few years. My grandmother used to accompany her preaching with singing accompanied by an autoharp and a flutina, a small keyboard instrument rather like an accordion but played sitting down and resting on the lap.

Five generations later my sons and their children are following in their great-great-grandparents' footsteps. My sister, married to an Anglican minister, has four sons who are also living in the blessing passed through the generations.

I have had the privilege of working with many songwriters over a number of years seeing praise and worship expand and grow in churches of different streams, coming together, often in great celebrations, to give us a taste of worship as we see it in Revelation.

With the proliferation of worship conferences, training schools, albums, YouTube videos and a whole number of resources from various publishers, the worship scene is now global. I know some have been critical and there is the danger of commercializing something that is essentially a spiritual activity, but never before in world history have countless worshippers been singing one song.

This must surely be a microcosm of what we read in Revelation.

Over the last fifty years I have been amazed at how songs travel around the world, and it is a sign of the global nature of the church that songs that we may associate with a particular group of churches or songwriters find their way into all kinds of situations.

I was once on holiday in Italy and visited the Catholic cathedral in Assisi. I was astonished to hear the song from the Eighties: 'Father, we love you, we worship and adore you, glorify your name in all the earth' being played on the magnificent cathedral organ, as the tourists and sightseers were walking around.

I heard that a group of monks in a monastery in Tibet had recorded my song 'Create in Me a Clean Heart' from Psalm 51.

Many current songwriters today have heard that their songs are being used in extraordinary circumstances. The magazine *Premier Christianity* reported an incident in Indonesia in 2015 when a group of prisoners faced a thirteen-man firing squad. They had been imprisoned for drug-trafficking but while in prison eight of the nine convicted had turned to Christ.

As the guns were fired, they were singing Matt Redman's song '10,000 Reasons'. Matt, reflecting on this incident, said:

> 'I don't think it gets more profound than that. Firstly, as a worship leader, that's the most amazing act of worship I've ever heard of. Secondly, it tells me you can face anything in this life and still be found with a song of worship on your lips, even a firing squad. And thirdly, I just thought: "How did that song end up there?"'[44]

This illustrates some of the themes in Revelation. The ability to face death, not loving their lives, but with worship on their lips.

Songs reach the world and it is important that songwriters are writing lyrics that are theologically sound, with a heart-warming expression!

Another story that shows how far songs travel and what can be accomplished through them concerns a song I wrote in 1986. We sang it at the Downs Bible Week.

This was an annual event for the New Frontiers family of churches led by Terry Virgo. It began in 1979 and over the next few years it had grown to such a degree that the week became two weeks. Thousands gathered from many nations to worship and hear teaching from the Bible. Every year there were many new songs and a worship album would be released. The song was called 'The Lord Has Displayed His Glory'.

It was included in the album but never really seemed to take off beyond the event. I had almost forgotten about it when, out of the blue, a couple of years later I had a phone call. It was from a Korean pastor who told me they sang my songs in his church in Seoul. It had a membership of several thousand and they were experiencing revival. One of the songs was the one I had forgotten about and shelved: 'The Lord Has Displayed His Glory'. I had never considered this to be one of my better songs and had dismissed it.

The Lord has displayed his glory
The kingdom is coming in power
The Spirit has come bringing life from the dead
How excellent is your name.
Hallelujah let your kingdom come
Let blind see, let the deaf hear
Let the lame man leap like a deer.
Jesus, we acclaim you
Lord of all creation
Bringing your kingdom to us now.
(Copyright ©1986 Thankyou Music)[45]

Apart from the Downs Bible Week and the album, I had never heard of anyone else singing it.

As the phone call progressed, he told me that they had been singing this song in their church and as it was being sung, what the song said began to happen: the blind were seeing, the deaf were hearing and the lame were walking. Revival was breaking out. Would I please come to Seoul and speak at a conference in the Olympic stadium? I remembered that when the news broke that the 1988 Olympic games were to be held in Seoul, I prophesied that a platform for the gospel and all that God was doing in the Korean church would come to the world's attention.

Now, four years after the song had been written, I was being asked to speak to 80,0000 in the very stadium I had prophesied about.

My ministry trip to Korea was lifechanging.

It began with me speaking at a conference for Taiwanese Christians on 'prayer mountain', a huge conference centre a few miles from Seoul, devoted to prayer. On approaching it, even in the car, the sound of prayer filled the air. There were prayer cells all over the huge complex with people crying to God. One section had been given over to praying for the UK, asking that God would send missionaries to the UK to evangelize it in its backslidden state. I felt totally challenged!

The sense of God's presence was so powerful that at times I could hardly stand up or speak.

After two days of ministry came the conference in the Olympic stadium where around 80,000 gathered. What happened there was the closest I have ever been to the worship described in Revelation.

There was a full orchestra with brilliant musicians, a huge choir, a conventional rock band with a worship leader and backing vocals and a visually stunning array of dancers. The sound of 80,000 voices accompanied by incredible musicians was a sensation that will live with me. There were times of hushed silence and then like the rush of a mighty waterfall the whole stadium would erupt in a majestic paean of praise. No football crowd could have reached a greater volume. When they prayed everyone prayed aloud together with a passion and fervency that left me breathless. The dancers moved with grace and beauty giving a wonderful artistic physical expression that prophetically spoke of all that God was doing and saying. Although the tonality and style of worship was universal, there was also a Korean worship team using their own ethnic instruments and playing and singing songs in the style of their own culture. The scales consisting of intervals and half semitones made it difficult for a Western musically trained ear, but this was natural to these people. Every tribe, tongue and nation took on a new meaning. The worship scene worldwide has much to learn!

There were salvations, healing, people filled with the Holy Spirit and deliverance from demonic strongholds. As I stepped up to the podium to speak, I could not believe I was there. It is the closest I have ever been to revival and it has given me a longing to see our sports stadia filled with people praising Jesus.

When I returned home, I could not sleep for a week. I could not stop praying and I wrote a whole album's worth of songs in just a few days. The album *Awaken the Nations* was the result. The memory lives on and the desire for God to do something like this in every nation still obsesses me.

I have recently seen a YouTube recording of this same song done by a Canadian First Nations church in their own language. This is thirty years on from when it was first written.

The Book of Revelation gives us a glimpse of our heavenly worship and the church needs to learn how to relate in its worship with every ethnic people group.

'Then I heard something like the voice of a great multitude and like the sound of many waters and like the sound of mighty peals of thunder, saying, "Hallelujah! For the Lord our God, the Almighty, reigns."' (Revelation 19:6 NASB)

Let us in these days, before Jesus comes back, seek to make our times of worship reflect the heavenly worship described in this glorious book.

CHAPTER 18
REVELATION, REVIVAL, RENEWAL, RESTORATION

The Book of Revelation gives us an overview of a fallen world and God's ultimate purpose in restoring it when Jesus returns, and the new heavens and new earth are reshaped without any sin, wars, disease or death.

God has never lost control and as we have seen chapter by chapter, his eternal plan has unfolded to bring hope and faith to encourage us to believe for a glorious future through all the changing scenes of history. The church is central to God's plan in seeing his kingdom reaching into all areas of life.

When Jesus taught the disciples to pray in what we often recite as the Lord's Prayer, he said: 'Your kingdom come, your will be done on earth as it is in heaven.' This is an eschatological prayer which will not be fully answered until Jesus comes again. However, the church does have a mandate to be an instrument of the kingdom in the present age.

Jesus demonstrated the power of the age to come by healing the sick, raising the dead, casting out demons and teaching. He taught, particularly through the Sermon on the Mount, the quality of life and holiness to which we can aspire.

The future kingdom was manifested in the presence of Jesus when he was on the earth. He commissioned his followers to carry on the mission of the kingdom after he was gone, and on the day of Pentecost when the Holy Spirit came in all his fullness and the church was birthed, a new age of the Spirit was inaugurated to carry on all that Jesus did and taught.

One of the indisputable prophetic signs Jesus said would happen before he returned was that the gospel of the kingdom would be preached to every nation (Matthew 24:14). The word 'nation' could be translated 'every ethnic people group'.

The Book of Acts, moving with incredible pace, saw the Early Church established. The proclamation of the gospel of the kingdom saw breakthroughs into the pagan world through the gospel message backed up with the same signs, wonders and miracles that Jesus had done.

In the midst of all the judgments and disasters of a fallen world that we have seen in the Book of Revelation, we also see the establishing of a people who have been cleansed from their sin and are now a kingdom and priests to God (Revelation 1:5-6). The NKJV translates these verses as: 'To Him who loved us and washed us from our sins in His own blood, and has made us kings and priests to His God and Father, to Him be glory and dominion forever and ever.' This makes this concept more personal, as well as corporate. We are personally kings and priests but there is a corporate expression of that through us being joined together as a people, the church. In 1 Peter chapter 2:9 we have his classic description of the church.

'But you are a chosen generation, a royal priesthood, a holy nation, His own special people, that you may proclaim the praises of Him who called you out of darkness into His marvellous light.' (NKJV)

When God created Adam, he made him to be a prophet, priest and king. Adam's sin meant he would lose those dimensions in which he could have lived his life.

Throughout the Old Testament the prophets, priests and kings were the ones anointed to represent the people to God and the spiritual life of the people of God was conducted through them. When Jesus came, he was the anointed Messiah, the prophet, priest and king 'par excellence'.

When the Holy Spirit was poured out on the day of Pentecost a new age was ushered in with the formation of the church, a people who would fulfil those prophetic, kingly, priestly roles which Adam lost.

Jesus, in his anointed Messianic role, fulfilled them perfectly and in his ascended glory continues to do so, but now the church as his body is to be a prophetic, priestly, kingly community representing him on the earth.

John indicates this very high view of the church in Revelation 1, but as we have already seen in Revelation 2 and 3 in the letters to the seven churches, even in the new covenant era, not everything was perfect about the way in which the newly formed churches responded.

However, Revelation not only teaches us about God's plan for the world and his outpourings of judgments because of its sinfulness; it teaches us what the church should be like, and can be like.

There have been times through 2,000 years of church history that after periods of decline, and characteristics reflecting those we have seen in the problems of the seven churches, that God has revived and renewed his church and there has been a sudden and dramatic growth spurt. This has often followed a period of repentance and much prayer, to bring the church back to her original intention.

These growth spurts or revivals were prophesied in Peter's sermon in Acts 3:19-21 when he took the opportunity to preach to the gathered crowd after healing the lame man at the Temple gate. He said:

'Repent therefore and be converted, that your sins may be blotted out, so that times of refreshing may come from the presence of the Lord, and that He may send Jesus Christ, who was preached to you before, whom heaven must receive until the times of restoration of all things, which God has spoken by the mouth of all His holy prophets since the world began.' (NKJV)

This is revival history encapsulated in a few words. It should give us hope as we read the Book of Revelation, that revival, renewal and restoration will happen alongside the judgments.

The outpouring of the Holy Spirit at the beginning of the twentieth century and the emergence of the Pentecostals, tended to polarize the evangelical world, since such spiritual gifts as tongues, prophecy, healing and other phenomena were not accepted by mainline evangelicals.

However, in the Sixties there was an outpouring of the Spirit that saw many traditional churches being renewed. The word 'renewal' was on many people's lips as the teaching of traditional Pentecostals infiltrated some of the bastions of Anglicanism, the Baptists, the Brethren and even more shockingly to some, the Catholics. The emphasis was placed on renewing the old!

However, new wine could not easily be contained in old wineskins and many began to break away and many new churches were formed. The Seventies and Eighties saw a tension between what became known as the 'charismatic movement' and traditional evangelicals.

The word 'renewal' began to evolve into 'restoration'. God was not about renewing old wineskins but restoring the church to its original intention, structures and ministries.

Fifty years on from the beginnings of the charismatic movement the body of Christ looks very different, with a greater unity and sense of purpose.

Whatever shade of evangelical opinion, there seems to be a hunger for something beyond what we are experiencing at the moment, however good it is. There does seem to be, even with different shades of opinion and practice, a much greater sense of unity in the body of Christ today than I have known in my lifetime.

However, the crying need throughout the world is the advance of the gospel, and that can only come about by a major outpouring of the Holy Spirit to bring revival.

My conclusion from my studies in Revelation is that the world will go on as it is until Jesus returns, but my other expectation is that there will be a glorious and powerful church that challenges the gross sinfulness of our generation and brings the love and mercy of God. I hope to see an evangelistic thrust where we will snatch people from the despair that sin brings, where we will build communities of love, where we can pray for the sick and see many healings, where we can hear the voice of God through his Word, where we can act like leaven by bringing truth and justice into society, where we can challenge racism, poverty and injustice, where we can restore family values and a right view of sexuality as God intended it and where we can infiltrate society with the values of the kingdom.

We know that light and darkness exist together until Jesus returns and Revelation tells that story. However, let us pray for the multitudes to be saved so that the great throng seen in heaven through John's amazing vision will be our eternal joy in the new heavens and earth, as together we gather around the throne to bring our worship to the eternal God, Creator Saviour, Deliverer, the Lamb slain, the Lion roaring and the Spirit breathing his life into every living soul.

POSTSCRIPT

Revelation is not an easy book, but it is vital in these days that we have an understanding of its message. It is a book which covers the whole gamut of Scripture through symbolism, statements, worship and challenge.

I am saddened that this is not a book that is preached on regularly and I challenge anyone who has responsibility for preaching and teaching God's word that this book be taken seriously. A proper understanding, as far as we are able, would solve much of the speculative prophetic conclusions held by some.

I totally believe in the gift of prophecy and the role of the prophet. But if prophetic insight is not based on the whole teaching of Scripture it is at best misleading and at worst false.

Our eschatological hope must be based on the overview of Scripture.

I end with a vision God gave me many years ago and which has been heightened recently while I have enjoyed many walks in the countryside. It is based on the question of what the world and the church will be like when Jesus returns.

A field of grass may be green throughout the year, but in the late spring it can be covered with buttercups. The field can either be seen as green or yellow. The grass is still there and is still green, but the glorious hue of the buttercups shines through. The Book of Revelation shows us that there will always be evil in the world and God's judgments will be poured out continually until Jesus returns. However, the bride is making herself ready, and adorning herself as God moves by his Spirit across the nations of the earth. In the midst of the darkness can we pray for a glorious church, shining with the radiance of his presence? The field of the world is green, but it is also alive with the glory of God's radiant church. Let us keep praying for revival and the radiance that overshadows the darkness.

It is time for the church to arise and shine.

The final prayer is 'COME QUICKLY, LORD JESUS.' AMEN, COME, LORD JESUS.

ENDNOTES

1. G.K. Beale and David H. Campbell, *Revelation: A Shorter Commentary* (William B. Eerdmans Publishing Co., 2015).

2. Gordon Fee, *How to Read the Bible for All Its Worth* (Zondervan, 2003).

3. G.K. Beale and David H. Campbell, *Revelation: A Shorter Commentary.*

4. G. Kittel, *Theological Dictionary of the New Testament* (William B. Eerdmans Publishing Co., 1965).

5. For a fuller development of the symbolism refer to G.K. Beale's *Revelation: A Shorter Commentary.*

6. Revelation 1:8 (NASB).

7. Revelation 1:5 (NIV).

8. Douglas Moo, *The Letters to the Colossians and Philemon* (Apollos, 2008).

9. Revelation 1:10 (NASB).

10. 'At Your Feet We Fall' written by David Fellingham. Copyright © 1982 Thankyou Music (adm. by CapitolCMGPublishing.com excl UK & Europe, adm. By Integrity Music, part of the David C. Cook Family, songs@integritymusic.com).

11. G.K. Beale and David H. Campbell, *Revelation: A Shorter Commentary.*

12. 'Build Your Church and Heal This Land' written by David Fellingham. Copyright © 1986 Thankyou Music (adm. by CapitolCMGPublishing.com excl. UK & Europe, adm. by Integrity Music, part of the David C. Cook family, songs@integritymusic.com).

13. G. Kittel, *Theological Dictionary of the New Testament.*

14. 'Crown Him With Many Crowns' written by Matthew Bridges (1800–1894).

15. 'Arise, My Soul, Arise' written by Charles Wesley (1707–1788).

16. Anthony A. Hoekema, *The Bible and the Future* (Paternoster Press, 1979).

17. G. Kittel, *Theological Dictionary of the New Testament*.

18. 'Keep the Touch of God on Your Soul' (author unknown).

19. G.K. Beale and David H. Campbell, *Revelation: A Shorter Commentary*.

20. G.K. Beale and David H. Campbell, *Revelation: A Shorter Commentary*.

21. 'Amazing Grace' written by John Newton (1725–1807).

22. G.K. Beale and David H. Campbell, *Revelation: A Shorter Commentary*.

23. D. Martyn Lloyd-Jones, *The Christian Warfare: An Exposition of Ephesians 6:10-13* (Baker Books, 1998).

24. G.K. Beale and David H. Campbell, *Revelation: A Shorter Commentary*.

25. 'Before the Throne of God Above' written by Vikki Cook and Charitie Bancroft. Copyright © 1997 Sovereign Grace Worship (adm. by CapitolCMGPublishing.com excl. UK & Europe, adm. by Integrity Music, part of the David C. Cook family, songs@integritymusic.com).

26. 'O Lamb of God' written by David Fellingham. Copyright © 1983 Thankyou Music (adm. by CapitolCMGPublishing.com excl. UK & Europe, adm. by Integrity Music, part of the David C. Cook family, songs@integritymusic.com).

27. Robert Letham, *Systematic Theology* (Crossway Books, 2019).

28. Revelation 19:6-7 (NASB).

29. 'Lo! He Comes with Clouds Descending' written by Charles Wesley (1707–1788).

30. Ralph Martin, *Worship in the Early Church* (Marshall, Morgan & Scott, 1964).

31. G. Kittel, *Theological Dictionary of the New Testament*.

32. Robert Letham, *Systematic Theology*.

33. William Hendrickson, *New Testament Commentary: John's Gospel* (Banner of Truth, 1959).

34. 'In Majesty He Comes' written by David Fellingham. Copyright © 1990 Thankyou Music (adm. by CapitolCMGPublishing.com excl. UK & Europe,

adm. by Integrity Music, part of the David C. Cook family, songs@integritymusic.com).

35. 'View of a Pig' by Ted Hughes, *Lupercal* (Faber & Faber, 1960).

36. 'Death is Nothing at All' by Henry Scott Holland (1847–1918).

37. Anthony A. Hoekema, *The Bible and the Future*.

38. Anthony A. Hoekema, *The Bible and the Future*.

39. Robert Letham, *Systematic Theology*.

40. G.K. Beale and David H. Campbell, *Revelation: A Shorter Commentary*.

41. Robert Letham, *Systematic Theology*.

42. G. Kittel, *Theological Dictionary of the New Testament*.

43. 'Beautiful Saviour' written by Stuart Townend. Copyright © 1998 Thankyou Music (adm. by CapitolCMGPublishing.com excl. UK & Europe, adm. by Integrity Music, part of the David C. Cook family, songs@integritymusic.com).

44. From *Premier Christianity* article by Joy Tibbs (June 2015).

45. 'The Lord Has Displayed His Glory' written by David Fellingham. Copyright © 1986 Thankyou Music (adm. by CapitolCMGPublishing.com excl. UK & Europe, adm. by Integrity Music, part of the David C. Cook family, songs@integritymusic.com).

Printed in Great Britain
by Amazon

57981031R00098